The Algonquin Round Table

Figure 1. Konrad Bercovici, 1940. *Source*: Mirana Comstock.

The Algonquin Round Table

25 Years with the Legends Who Lunch

KONRAD BERCOVICI

Edited by

MIRANA COMSTOCK

EXCELSIOR
EDITIONS

Cover Credit: The Algonquin Round Table (New York), c.1923. Author Konrad Bercovici stands with Burton Rascoe, observing fellow Algonquinites, seated, clockwise from left: Hendrik van Loon, Dorothy Parker, Joseph Kaufman, Alexander Woollcott, Horace Liveright, Franklin P. Adams, Marc Connelly, Johnny Weaver, Heywood Broun, Robert Benchley; standing, Robert Sherwood, and host Frank Case. Caricature by Bill Breck.

Published by State University of New York Press, Albany

© 2024 State University of New York

Excelsior Editions is an imprint of State University of New York Press

For information, contact State University of New York Press, Albany, NY
www.sunypress.edu

Library of Congress Cataloging-in-Publication Data

Names: Bercovici, Konrad, 1882–1961, author. | Comstock, Mirana, editor.
Title: The Algonquin Round Table : 25 years with the legends who lunch / Konrad Bercovici ; edited by Mirana Comstock.
Description: Albany, NY : State University of New York Press, [2024] | Series: Excelsior editions.
Identifiers: LCCN 2023042711 | ISBN 9781438497235 (pbk. : alk. paper) | ISBN 9781438497242 (ebook)
Subjects: LCSH: Algonquin Round Table. | Authors, American—New York (State)—New York—20th century—Biography. | Bercovici, Konrad, 1882–1961.
Classification: LCC PS129 .B43 2024 | DDC 810.9/0052—dc23/eng/20240102
LC record available at https://lccn.loc.gov/2023042711

10 9 8 7 6 5 4 3 2 1

Contents

Illustrations

Foreword

Mirana Comstock

My mother liked to tell this story. So do I.

One sunny Sunday afternoon, on a bus heading up New York's Riverside Drive, she overheard a fellow passenger observe, "There goes an oak tree out walking with a daisy." She then caught sight of what they were observing—a striking, peasant-sturdy older gentleman with a big mustache, holding hands with a blonde little girl as they crossed from Riverside Park and disappeared into an apartment building facing it.

He was my grandpa, Konrad Bercovici. I was that daisy.

Like some sort of creative commune, for much of my childhood, my mother, brother, grandparents, aunt, and I all shared an apartment in that building. Most of the rooms overlooked the park, Hudson River, and George Washington Bridge beyond. The ever-changing views of water and sky were considered essential, not only for painting, but also for your brain to breathe when writing, composing, playing music, or just thinking.

Do not disturb signs were frequently posted on the closed doors of the apartment's rooms. And although everyone was quite communicative—so many stories to tell!—you never bothered anyone while they were working. The thundering chords emanating from grandpa's Hammond organ did not count as a disturbance. It was, after all, Bach. This respect for work had a practical side, too. From a very young age, my mother, Mirel and her sister, Rada, had come to think of stories as currency. If they wanted something, they didn't see why their father couldn't just write and sell a couple more stories and make it happen. Which he usually did.

Figure 2. Bercovici with his daughter, Mirel, as a young artist. *Source*: Mirana Comstock.

An internationally acclaimed writer, journalist, and historian, Konrad Bercovici authored forty books, hundreds of short stories, plays, screenplays, magazine and newspaper articles. All while raising four brilliant, highly independent children with my grandmother, Naomi, and maintaining households in Hollywood, New York, Connecticut, and Paris. I really can't figure out how he did it. Sure, no TV. But I also remember my mother telling me grandpa just didn't need the same amount of sleep as other people did. When he was younger, he would get up early and go dance in the woods to burn off excess energy without waking up his sleeping family. It's funny to imagine him out there in the wee hours, head back, barrel chest thrust forward, arms and legs flung about. What did the animals think?

When he wasn't writing stories, grandpa was telling them. My brother—"Little Konrad," as opposed to his namesake, "Big Konrad"—and

I would snuggle up to him, enraptured. Far too lively to be bedtime stories, if anything, they kept us awake and probably also laid the groundwork for my becoming a writer. That, and with three generations of artists in the family, there was simply no wall space left by the time I came along. Not that everyone didn't also write. I was convinced our veins were blue because there was ink in them. Unfortunately, I shared that theory with my third-grade science class one time.

A large mahogany double-doored deco cabinet we called "The Tarambula" occupied a wall in the living room of our apartment. I'm not sure if it had that name before it was moved from my grandparents' home in Ridgefield, Connecticut, to Riverside Drive. I'm also not sure what it really means. Googling yields a bird, some guy in Ukraine, and a girl's first name representing spirituality. It now resides in my home, outside Boston. And it's still called "The Tarambula." As the last of my branch of the family, it contains most of the papers I inherited from them.

When I finally start to go through these papers—my dislike for anything resembling filing or organizing another inherited trait—I begin to get a firsthand look at my grandpa's seemingly endless supply of that family ink. In addition to his impressive body of published work, there are also thousands of pages of unpublished manuscripts—books, stories, articles, plays, even reality series concepts! There are photographs with Mary Pickford and Douglas Fairbanks on the back lot, Charlie Chaplin and Paulette Goddard at the theatre, Louis Nizer and Joe DiMaggio around the Algonquin Round Table. My favorite, however, is one in which you hardly even see grandpa—he's a tiny speck in a white suit, lecturing thousands of troops during World War II about the dangers of Hitler and the Nazis.

There is also lots of writing about his writing—hundreds of laudatory reviews and interviews in crumbling newsprint from all over the world. The *New York Times* hailing Konrad Bercovici as "a master romancer future generations will rank with Chekhov and Maupassant"; famed short story editor Edward J. O'Brien calling him "America's master of the short story"; John Reed, who wrote the introduction to grandpa's first book, *Crimes of Charity*, declaring his "literary power of absolute conviction."

At first, I tried hard to resist reading the manuscripts themselves. If you started, you just couldn't put them down and ended up reading instead of filing or organizing. But then again, that is how I discovered the unpublished work. A romantic novel set against the gentrification of Greenwich Village in the 1950s. Memoir stories about a circle that included Chaplin, Hemingway, Dreiser, Fitzgerald, Einstein—so many luminaries who called him friend, collaborator, mentor and, at times, brutally honest critic. And, ultimately, *The Algonquin Round Table*, an insider's view of the legendary place many of these luminaries thought of as their home away from home.

I remember when grandpa would go to the Algonquin for lunch. Usually in a suit, sometimes with a Gypsy-red shirt under the jacket. Always with a smile so big, even that mustache couldn't hide it. Reading *The Algonquin Round Table*, I feel as if I am lunching there with him and that golden era's incredible Who's Who of fellow guests. Reading the family papers—"The Konrad Bercovici Story"—I realize how closely the romance and adventure of his life and work are intertwined.

As the *New York Times* headlined, on the loss of one of their own, "Journalist, film writer, author . . . the romanticism of his career was reflected in his work . . . Konrad Bercovici was a writer of great gusto. A world traveler who enriched his writing talent in the tradition of the determined journeyman of life." And what a journey it was!

The Konrad Bercovici Story

Konrad Bercovici (1881–1961) was born on a boat on the Bosphorus, not far from the Danube, and raised in the Romanian port town of Braila. His father was an agriculturist and horse breeder. His mother, a talented singer, violinist, and storyteller, encouraged her son's love of music and writing. He spent much of his early years in Gypsy camps and caravans, playing violin in their bands and wandering from fair to fair. By the time he reached his teens, there were few European countries Konrad Bercovici didn't know, as one can only truly know a land or a people: on foot. He spoke many of their languages, too, including Gypsy Calo, Greek, Romanian, French, German, Italian, Turkish, and Yiddish.

Originally intending to be a musician, he eventually made his way to Paris to study with Albert Schweitzer's teacher, organist and composer Charles Maria Widor, at The Madeleine. While in Paris, he became associated with the Montparnasse literary group led by Anatole France and developed friendships with fellow countryman Brâncuși and his assistant, Modigliani, whose sketch of Bercovici is in MoMA's permanent collection. He also fell in love and eloped with artist Naomi LiBrescu, who would become the mother of his four children and creative soul mate for more than sixty years.

Figure 3. Konrad Bercovici in Gypsy attire. *Source*: Mirana Comstock.

Emigrating to New York's lower East Side in 1904, Konrad Bercovici found a city bustling with exciting people and new ideas. But not a lot of jobs for musicians. He barely supported his young family as a manual laborer, charity investigator, and piano player at a nickelodeon. His expertise in music eventually led to a job as music critic for the *New York Sun*. He also began writing colorful stories for the Sunday edition about the vibrant ethnic neighborhoods of his new home and the Gypsy camps of his old one, splitting the ten-dollar payment with illustrators George Bellows and John Sloan. His first book, *Crimes of Charity*, a bitter indictment of the indifference of the organizations he had investigated, was published in 1917.

Work for *The Nation* and the *New York Times* followed, then a job as a reporter for *The World*. Continuing to write stories for magazines, as well as newspapers, Bercovici's name was soon heralded simultaneously on the covers of multiple editions of such popular publications as *Esquire*,

Harper's, The Dial, Century, Atlantic Monthly, Collier's, Liberty, McCall's, Woman's Home Companion, and the *Ladies' Home Journal* at newsstands across the country.

This unique combination of romantic storyteller and hard-nosed journalist caught the eye of legendary publisher Horace Liveright, who subsequently published many of Konrad Bercovici's early books. After starting the enormously popular Modern Library series to bring great literature to the masses—the paperbacks of their day—Liveright had founded a publishing house with the foresight to discover and help launch the careers of, in addition to Bercovici, such authors as Theodore Dreiser, F. Scott Fitzgerald, Eugene O'Neill, William Faulkner, Sherwood Anderson, and, after Bercovici introduced them, Ernest Hemingway. Even after their careers took them in different directions, this elite group still sought each other out for camaraderie, intellectual stimulation, a chance to be themselves away from the limelight.

Konrad Bercovici went on to publish more than forty critically acclaimed books for other top publishers, including best-selling novels, biographies, and still-quoted historical and sociological works on every-thing from *The Crusades* to *The Story of the Gypsies*. Considered a primary reference work on the subject to this day, the *New York Times* wrote in its review of the latter, "Konrad Bercovici is to be taken as authority on a subject so elusive that he stands practically alone, a monopolist of learning . . . Bercovici has written a book for future reference as well as immediate pleasure."

During the golden age of the genre, Konrad Bercovici also con-tinued to write and publish hundreds of short stories, including more multi-starred selections in O'Brien's famed *Best Short Stories of the World* collection than any other author. The critics were equally laudatory—even the dubious ones. "I couldn't help resenting Edward J. O'Brien's statement that Konrad Bercovici was America's master of the short story," wrote Ring Lardner. "However, resentment lessened a great deal as I read the stories in Mr. Bercovici's *Iliana* . . . They are all beautifully written . . . I like *Iliana* a lot."

The Nation hailed *Ghitza and Other Romances of Gypsy Blood* as "superb gypsy tales . . . the psychology of his characters is both subtle and convincing. Truth and nature are married to legend and beauty and the result is one of the most charming and stirring of all recent books." And the *New York Times* wrote of his story collection *Murdo*, "Poetry, romance and passion form its very essence." One of the stories from that collection, "The Death of Murdo," was culled from more than 10,000 stories to make the final list for 1999's Updike-edited *Best American Short Stories of the Century*. According to the book's introduction, the Romania-based story was only eliminated due to a space-saving cut of those not taking place in America.

As a playwright and, when Hollywood came calling, a screenwriter, Bercovici also worked with Cecil B. DeMille, Edwin Carewe, and Victor Fleming, as well as penning the original script for *The Great Dictator* for Charlie Chaplin. The subject of a celebrated plagiarism suit, with noted attorney Louis Nizer successfully representing plaintiff Bercovici, it was covered extensively by news media around the world.

In an early book dedication to Chaplin, Bercovici had written: "Dear Charlie, the last part of this book was written in your studio. A good many things in it I told you while we were trying to reveal ourselves to each other, tearing the masks away which we present to those to whom we refuse ourselves. In wishing *Murdo* godspeed, I cannot help thinking of you as one of the fraternity that serenades at empty windows. Love from your Konrad."

Figure 4. Charlie Chaplin and Bercovici on the set of *The Gold Rush*. *Source*: Mirana Comstock.

My mother had typed the original treatment for the film. Family friend Melvyn Douglas had witnessed Bercovici acting out the story for Chaplin at his Pebble Beach home. Chaplin was even my aunt's godfather, changing her given name from Revolte to Rada on her sixteenth birthday. The betrayal of such a close personal and professional relationship came as a terrible shock to the entire family. But with a world once more on the brink of war, there were other things to think about.

From the wit of *The Great Dictator* to incisive reporting on corruption in Romania that led to a savage beating by the Iron Guard, Bercovici had never turned his back on journalism or politics. And with some sort of uncanny news sense—Gypsy intuition?—he always seemed to be there when stories were unfolding: Lindbergh's landing in Paris; revolution in Austria; the king's abdication during the Spanish Civil War. And now, as the *Herald Tribune* observed, Bercovici "was one of the first writers to spot the trend of Hitler and Nazism and the peril to democracy and Western civilization."

After interviewing Goebbels and Goering and witnessing the horror of Hitler's public spectacles at the Sportspalast, Bercovici could not go back and write the romantic stories his publisher and readers were clamoring for. Instead, he continued to investigate and write about the rise of fascism, including an account of the growing Nazi Bund movement in America, *Undercover*, written under a pseudonym to protect his sources—and his life. And, when World War II broke out, he joined the war department's orientation bureau, lecturing thousands of soldiers across the country about the threat both here and abroad.

Later, when escaping Jews from Germany sought to enter Palestine and were turned back by the British, he became a leader of the free Palestine movement, cofounding *The Answer* magazine and serving on its editorial board alongside Albert Einstein. Settling his plagiarism suit against Chaplin—after seven years of delays—in order to have the financial means to buy ammunition and medicine, he joined the Irgun in Israel, alongside Moshe Dayan and Menachem Begin, who became lifelong friends. "Konrad Bercovici, the great writer, supported the fight for liberation of our people with unsurpassed civil courage. I cherish his memory with all my heart," Begin wrote, after his death.

In subsequent years, Konrad Bercovici continued to publish such well-received works as *Savage Prodigal*, a biography of the poet Verlaine, and the biblically themed Book-of-the-Month-Club selection *The Exodus*. "Konrad Bercovici's kaleidoscopic narrative, *The Exodus*, is written in the cadences of the Old Testament, presented as a series of colorful, stylized scenes in which the effect is almost that of ideograms carved on a tower or on a temple wall, picturing the story of an old adventure," the *New York Times* wrote. "These accounts are sufficiently expanded to bring increased humanity to individuals. Throughout, the author has kept in mind the parallel between this early story and conditions today. Anti-Semitism in Egypt of the fifteenth century B.C. has all the passion and illogic that it has in the twentieth century A.D."

As he moved into his seventies, many of Bercovici's earlier books continued to be translated and widely published around the world, as were his stories, appearing in numerous anthologies and "best of" collections here and abroad. He had a syndicated newspaper column and sat on the board of *Prevent World War III* magazine, spoke at numerous public events, and appeared on television panels alongside such authors as Norman Mailer. A member of the famed Algonquin Round Table since the days of Heywood Broun, Dorothy Parker, and Franklin P. Adams, he lunched there daily. And, prolific as always, he continued to write . . . and write . . . and write.

In December 1961, as news spread around the world of Konrad Bercovici's passing, crowds gathered in New York, and the streets around the funeral home had to be closed to traffic. The famous came, but so did the readers, some clutching well-worn copies of his books and stories that had continued to resonate with them through the years.

"All of us, and that includes thousands of people throughout the world, have suffered the most painful and irreplaceable loss," Louis Nizer wrote. "I have met a number of great men and Konrad was, of course, a great man, but never did I meet such a rare man. He was rare in the extraordinary accumulation of knowledge in so many variegated fields of life that it stunned the imagination to contemplate it. We all sat at his feet to learn and marvel . . . If I have to count the blessings of my life, high upon the list, if not indeed first, would be the privilege of being with him for perhaps a quarter of a century at daily luncheons."

Back at the family apartment on Riverside Drive, a tall gentleman with piercing black eyes appeared, violin in hand. He entered, without saying a word, then proceeded to play the most beautiful, heart-wrenching Gypsy music. An hour later, he stopped, wiped the tears from his eyes, and left, just as suddenly and mysteriously as he had arrived. But the music still hung in the air. And continues to, waiting for new readers to hear it through the work of master storyteller Konrad Bercovici.

Introduction

In the British Museum, in London, there are several clay tablets three thousand and more years old, originally sent by a Babylonian merchant to his son traveling on business.

"Be careful of the people you associate with," the father warned his son, "and don't trust such as claim to be your friends. Be careful also of the food you eat and the wine you drink and the women you associate with. It was different in my young days, when I was sent by my father to act for him in strange cities. Then the food was fresh, the wine was undiluted and the innkeepers honest. In those days people were true and honest, and those who called themselves one's friends could be banked on."

This is but a brief extract from the Babylonian's long message to his son. If one could find the clay tablets sent by this son to his son, and from that son to his son down, from father to son, down to the present day, the warnings would read the same as the first one.

"In my young days . . ."

∼

Nostalgia, almost always coupled with distrust, is part of the nature of man everywhere, from time immemorial. The long, bronze-tipped spear of the Macedonian phalanges under Alexander, an improvement over the shorter, iron-tipped spear used by the armies of his father, Philip, were denounced fiercely by the old generals because they robbed war of its glamour.

"The longer weapon," wrote Epaminondas, one of the great generals, "wins battles but robs the warrior of the feel of bravery he would have felt handling a shorter one in contact with the enemy."

When firearms were first used in war, the older soldiers protested. It was, they said, "uninspiring" to kill an enemy outside personal combat, "corps-à-corps."

Some of our older generals are now denouncing radar and the atomic bomb for taking "the heart" out of war. "The machine is the hero," they complain.

The papyrus was denounced by the generation that had used clay tablets, just as the use of phonetics and letters was decried by the users of hieroglyphics, and the art of printing was denounced as the end of the calligraphic art, the "flower of civilization," and the vulgarization of learning.

Civilization progresses in zig-zag fashion, but progresses nevertheless, mechanically, culturally, yet every older generation believes itself superior to the younger one; and when it cannot claim superior knowledge or comfort, it lays claim to superior wisdom, well-being, and glamour.

∾

I remember the day my father brought the first kerosene lamp to our home and hung it on the wall. It was a great innovation. It gave more light than ten candles. Some of our Moslem neighbors came to our door and said that it was not right to change night into day, to change what the Lord had ordained, and were all for compelling the household to go back to the wax candle. We did. Today there is electricity in the same village.

"In my young days . . ."

This glamorizing of the past represents a desire to hold back time by reliving one's own youth, claiming for it joys and advantages, having forgotten the bitter and the ashes.

There isn't an old man who wouldn't tell you that in his younger days the women were fairer and that the meat and the fruit tasted better than they do today; forgetting, of course, that his own father had said the same thing about the women, the meat, and the fruit he had had in his young days.

"Oh, for grandmother's cooking . . ."

"Oh, for the old wines . . ."

∾

The pendulum of man's soul oscillates between the instincts of self-preservation and self-destruction. To glamorize the immediate past is to give up one's own youth and to hasten one's end. Regrets and nostalgia are more responsible for wrinkles on the face and sagging of the flesh than time. The men and women who have stayed young are the ones who set their sails windward, without looking back with longing to the shores left behind.

~

There was a Round Table in the Rose Room of the Algonquin Hotel. Many of the men and women who had lunched daily about that table were already nationally famous in all the branches of literature, or eventually became so.

In the course of twenty-five years that the table had been their daily gathering place, some of the ones who had lent great éclat had died, including Alexander Woollcott, Heywood Broun, Robert Benchley, Hendrik Willem van Loon, John Touhey, Ring Lardner, and Beatrice Kaufman. The others—Marc Connelly, Robert Sherwood, Deems Taylor, Dorothy Parker, Laurence Stallings, and Gene Fowler—eventually went west in search of greener pastures, and Franklin P. Adams, the beloved F. P. A., Edna Ferber, George Kaufman, and Harold Ross are probably finding reunion at the same table too replete with memories to gather about it. When they do come, they come singly and sit at separate tables most of the time.

As a group, they represented what was most conspicuous in those days. They were able men and women in their respective fields, and were colorful. They were, in their own way, like the group in Paris known as *les grands tapageurs*. Benchley's hilarity, Broun's pugnacious columns, Woollcott's and Ward Moorehouse's fearless criticism, Deems Taylor's music, Sherwood's, Kaufman's, Connelly's, and Ferber's plays were new and startling in America. *Beggar on Horseback*, *Butter and Egg Man*, *The Royal Family*, *Green Pastures*, *The Petrified Forest*, *The Man Who Came to Dinner*, and *Reunion in Vienna* were startling innovations.

Ring Lardner's originality, van Loon's learning and quipping, and F. P. A.'s stabbing lines were way out of the ordinary and made people sit up and take notice. Dorothy Parker's bon mots had wings. Within twenty-four hours they had flown from lip to lip, were embedded in type, quoted, and repeated, and became part of the folklore of the literati and cognoscenti—not without the help of Frank Case's friends, the columnists. The columnists were originally small-town newspapermen who brought the "personals" to the big city. When Dorothy Parker hadn't said anything witty in a long time, some clever fellow invented something that sounded as if she might have said it. It helped keep the reputation of the Algonquin Round Table's smartness in good standing, active, and an attraction.

Many people lunched in the Rose Room to see the famous and perhaps hear what they said, as much as they came to eat. And since the Round Tablers themselves were young and splendid showmen, they enjoyed being seen and admired, despite their seeming detachment from the hoi polloi. They made entrances and exits at the Algonquin. They made people aware that they were somebodies. The waiters took their cue from Case and made a great fuss over them. There wasn't a shrinking violet in the lot. Woollcott, Broun, Benchley, Connelly, and Kaufman, to name only a few, eventually acted on the stage and in the movies, in plays about themselves, or in their own plays.

~

During the life of the Rose Room Round Table, another group of people lunched daily together in the Oak Room. Frank Case used to refer to it as the "Soap Box." The more perspicacious headwaiter, Raul, who used to and still does lend an attentive ear to the discussions at that table, calls it "The Academy."

While literature in all its branches was the chief topic in the Rose Room—literature and the gossip about writers, editors, publishers, directors, and producers—around the Oak Room table, the discussions hovered between local, national, and international politics, economics and philosophy, law and the sciences, with literature and the other arts thrown in for good measure.

Since the dissolution of the Rose Room Round Table, many new things have come into being, with which they hadn't had to concern themselves. World War II. Radar. Television. The atomic bomb. Nuclear physics. Literature, per se, has been somewhat relegated to the rear.

The constants at the Oak Room table are Lou Nizer, Dr. Frank Kingdon, Jack Alicoate, Martin Quigley, Harry Hershfield, William G. O'Brien, Elmer Leterman, and myself. Unlike what happened in the Rose

Figure 5. The Algonquin Rose Room. At the table are Louis Nizer, Harry Hershfield, Konrad Bercovici, Joe DiMaggio, Ben Bodne, and Abel Green. *Source*: Courtesy Michael Colby.

Room, guests are not frowned upon, but they are generally of a caliber at least equal to the constants. When a guest like Dr. Hyman Goldsmith, the eminent nuclear physicist, is there, he is plied with questions about nuclear physics. When a diplomat like Clark Griffith lunches at that table, the questions asked are of national and international importance. Dr. Amadeo Gianini, the banker, is questioned on financial matters, psychiatrists on their subjects, and biologists on theirs. An array of men prominent in all walks of life, in every phase of culture—novelists, philosophers, priests, judges, ministers, rabbis, generals, mayors of cities, police chiefs, actors, producers, directors, newspaper columnists, and television technicians—succeed each other.

Lou Nizer, with his best courtroom technique, is always first to question the witness. Suave, he elicits answers to questions his witness is not prepared to answer.

"If I am not indiscreet, would you please tell us whether, in your opinion, the Russians are as well advanced in nuclear physics as they say they are?"

Or, to John Rogge, the prosecuting attorney in the case of the subversive group which was dropped by the authorities after the death of the judge:

"Why was the case dropped? Lack of evidence or a weak stomach?"

And Rogge, embarrassed, answering that in the light of what he has since learned, the case should never have been tried.

And if a guest attempts to make others believe that he knows more than he really does, Frank Kingdon is right on top of him to prove him out of his own depth; for there is little that Frank hasn't looked into with keen eyes and delved deeply with his splendidly equipped mind. He raises his sword with a laugh, like a gay warrior, and proceeds to puncture the other one's armor full of holes. Frank's motto is: "No Sham."

Harry Hershfield has an apropos story on every subject. He can make the dictionary read like a joke book. What one hears him tell over the air are pale copies of strong originals.

Jack Alicoate holds the reins, is the moderator, and sees that no one monopolizes a discussion.

"Now, we've heard you. Let somebody else have a go at this man."

Jack is a pessimistic capitalist. He is an anti-communist, but is afraid that some form of communism is going to engulf us and the world, and only hopes it is held off while he is alive.

Elmo Roper, the pollster who so blithely predicted the defeat of President Truman, was made to give an account, not of his false prediction, but of the manner of getting the information on which his prediction was based.

"Are polls wind waves or wind tunnels?" Jack asked.

"Isn't what is in the mind of the questioner guiding the answers?" Lou Nizer wanted to know. And a third one quoted: "Since polls have failed to predict the trend on such important events as national elections, by their present methods, are the pollsters going to change their methods?"

"What about big business? What is their reaction to your wrong guesses?"

Martin Quigley, who knows more about theological history than a college professor, expounds his knowledge in slow, measured sentences that sound as if conceived in medieval Latin, though he uses the most colloquial English.

John G. O'Brien, who has spent many years in government service, abroad, is the European expert.

Radio companies have repeatedly offered to put those daily discussions on the air, but by general assent the offers were refused, chiefly because the table would be robbed of its spontaneity; because everybody would be self-conscious, and conscious that he was talking to millions of people, instead of a dozen or so. When appropriate, no one hesitates to use strong language. Television, too, has made its offer and been refused.

Bromides and bores are not invited a second time.

A list of the names of all the people who have participated in the discussions of the Oak Room Round Table would be like the roster of an encyclopedia. The men in the Oak Room are far from being of one opinion on any subject: literary, political, or economic. Strong personalities, they argue heatedly with whoever differs with their views, but without acrimony. Twenty years of threshing out their opinions and beliefs with each other has not disturbed the personal harmony among people poles apart in opinions, and of different races, backgrounds, faiths, and cultures. It could only happen in the U.S.A.

I venture to say that in some future day, a distant future day, I hope, people will speak of the Oak Room Round Table with the same nostalgia they are now speaking of the Rose Room table.

"Where are the snows of yesteryear?"

The Algonquin Round Table

At the beginning of the century, when Frank Case took over the Algonquin Hotel from its previous owners, it was just another one of several
second-rate hotels in the neighborhood. Forty-Second Street had not
yet become the pivot of the city. The theatres had only begun the move
uptown. Most of the daily newspapers were published around Park Row,
close to the Brooklyn Bridge; the offices of many monthly magazines and
book publishing companies were still downtown, and actors, writers and
playwrights, directors and producers didn't foregather as they do now, in
any one particular place.

Taking into consideration the economic conditions of the majority
of actors and writers of those days, some forty-odd years ago, one realizes that very few of the fraternity earned enough to eat in any but the
cheapest restaurants and live in any but the cheapest garrets in town. The
popular notion that the gentry of the arts starved in garrets was much
closer to the truth than is generally admitted.

Except for a few fortunate mortals, writing was not a paying profession in those days. The coin was in posthumous honors after a Potter's
Field burial. When the editor of a magazine accepted a story, an article,
or even a serial novel for publication, he never followed the acceptance
with a check. Writers were only paid after publication, which frequently
meant a year, and sometimes two, and the amount of the check was
usually what the editor felt like paying at the moment. Few were told
how much they would eventually get and when. To get something on
account, authors had to harass the editors, cashiers, and publishers and
sit on their doorsteps.

When a story or a novel was sold for publication to a magazine,
all rights were included; a condition that made it possible for *Munsey's*

to sell the movie rights to all the stories published for years in their magazine for a huge flat sum to a Hollywood motion picture company, without giving the authors any part of the money it received, and to sell the second serial rights to second-rate magazines on the same conditions. I know, because it happened to me.

With the exception of two or three dime novels, Horatio Alger stories and the like, authors of very good, or popular novels, starved when they didn't have a side occupation. Some were janitors, others were tailors, jewelers, schoolteachers, and one of our greatest poets chopped tickets at an elevated railroad station in Brooklyn.

The playwrights of the day were only a little better off. Most of the plays produced back then were concocted within a few days, and their authors were either on the payroll of the company, on a weekly salary, or sold their plays outright to the producer. They were the real slaves of the pen.

Actors had not yet banded together in a union. The very few at the top earned enough to live riotously and permit themselves the luxury of carriages, plumed ladies, diamond buttons on their frilled shirts, and homes in the country; but the majority of the thespians lived from hand to mouth, lunching and dining in beer saloons that offered free food of a sort with the drinks. Hamlet's soliloquy was heard only too often in barrooms on Saturday nights, when the hat was passed. Actors also frequently had other occupations, not only between plays, but also to fill out their days.

The overall economic and social position of the whole fraternity of the graphic and stage arts was still at its lowest ebb. Many years passed before some of the newspapers instituted daily columns for book reviews and theatrical and musical criticism. And still more years passed before the doings of writers, actors, directors, and editors, save for an occasional scandal, became sufficiently important to the readers to be mentioned in print.

Neither writer, musician, nor actor had any standing in the community. They were still considered bohemians, and had made only an inconsiderable step from the beginning of the nineteenth century, when they were required to use the servants' staircase when going to see their patrons, and were still frowned upon by the church.

There were hotels and cafés in New York frequented by the elite of the community, however that elite was not composed of the intellectuals, but of big businessmen, bankers, merchants, stockbrokers, railroad men, and politicians. People gathered at the Brevoort and the Lafayette, at Rector's, Mouquin's, Sherry's, the Holland House, and Chauncey's Tavern to discuss business and politics. When they did talk about writers and the stage, it was only in connection with some recent scandal, or to compare the beauty of this or that recent toast of the stage with the ones of previous years.

The wits were not Dorothy Parker, Alexander Woollcott, Heywood Broun, or George Kaufman, Louis Nizer, and Frank Kingdon, but the Crockers, the Murphys, the Platts, and other such as gathered at the "Amen Corner."

$\sim$

The more literary of the plays were first produced by the foreign theatres downtown. Long before Ibsen's plays had made their bow on Broadway, they had been produced at the Thalia Theatre on the Bowery, the Grand Street Theatre on Grand Street, in Yiddish, Russian, Italian, and German, and the Garibaldi on Fourth Street and Second Avenue. Tolstoy's, Chekhov's, and Gorky's plays were first produced by the Armenian theatre, downtown. The German theatre on Irving Place, directed at the time by Mady Christians's father, Rudolph, was the first to intersperse an occasional play by Strindberg or Schnitzler into the usual tingle-tangle that was being presented day in, day out, to amuse the theatregoers to whom "Die Schnitzelbank" was the sauerkraut of dramatic art.

The first serious effort towards an intellectual American theatre in New York was made by the Provincetown Players. In a theatre that had been a stable the year before, the plays of O'Neill, John Reed, and Floyd Dell were first produced, as well as plays by Synge and Shaw first seeing the light of day. From there eventually emerged the Greenwich Village Playhouse, and later, the Theatre Guild, whose founders seceded from it and moved uptown to what had been the "Vieux Colombier Theatre" of a visiting French company financed by the late Otto Kahn. His interest in the theatre had first manifested itself when he paid for the upholstering of the seats of the Provincetown Theatre on Mulberry Street.

Needless to say, the remuneration of the actors and playwrights of the intellectual theatre was so meagre, Sunday breakfast at the Brevoort or the Lafayette was a great luxury, made possible by dispensing with lunch for two or three days. Though these artists made Greenwich Village famous, and the real estate owners and agents wealthy, the better apartments were occupied by outsiders who craved color and atmosphere and a fling at free love, and not by the ones who created that color and atmosphere. When garrets in the Village became fashionable, the real estate agents rented them to fashionable people who hired interior decorators to "age" the new antiques, and the artists, writers, and actors had to be content with dark basements for the rent they could pay. In time, even basements were beyond their means.

While this intellectual ferment was at a boiling point below Forty-Second Street, the plays most in vogue in the uptown theatrical district were *Bertha, the Sewing Machine Girl*, *The Great Divide*, and such concoctions as the hired-by-the-week playwrights provided, several of whom proved later on how much better they could do under more favorable conditions.

To be sure, there were thespians with great ability, ambition, and talent, and there was never a season in which some of Shakespeare's plays were not presented. But again, with the exception of the great stars, frequently imported from England, the compensation of the other actors was lower than that of the plumber, carpenter, bricklayer, and even the street cleaner, and their social standing was not as good.

∽

I am telling all this in an attempt to depict the conditions prevalent when the Algonquin came into being and welcomed artists under its roof. It was out of the meeting of kindred souls in the arts that organizations grew to protect the protagonists of the arts economically, to give them stature, to make it possible for them to live like respectable human beings, and in so doing, to root their position in our society. To permit them to raise families, educate their children, and do away with the stigma of bohemianism that had clung to them for centuries and made them carry their talents like crosses.

It was because actors found a place to meet and talk and discuss their lot that Equity came into being and acting became an honored profession. It now seems unbelievable that some of our great stars should have been so ungenerous and blind as to oppose an actor's union, to vilify them when they struck for a living.

It is because writers had a place to get together, talk over their troubles, and discuss their conditions that the Author's League was able to fight the iniquity that compelled writers to hand over the product of their brains, time, and talent to an editor who didn't think it necessary to tell them when payment for the work would be forthcoming, or how much that payment would be. It was taken for granted that an author had to live in a garret, starve, wear threadbare clothes, and trudge on shoes down-at-the-heel. A genius, to be a genius, first had to die of starvation and be buried in Potter's Field.

It would be an overstatement to say that artist organizations came into existence solely because the Algonquin existed. Any other place where they could have met might have brought about the same result, but one has a right to suppose that the friendly atmosphere created by Frank Case's hotel contributed to the speeding up of the process.

In retrospect, it hardly seems possible that such conditions existed only a few decades ago. The story of Edgar Allan Poe's poverty is now too well known for anyone to dwell on, but one should keep in mind that whatever the social and economic conditions of Poe, they were almost brilliant compared with what most of the writers living and writing in his time had to put up with in New York, as well as in other centers. After all, Poe was a famous writer while he lived. Even so, his translators got more for their efforts than he had gotten for his. If he starved on what he earned by his pen, what about the less famous!

John O'Hara Cosgrave, who edited *The Wave* in San Francisco in the first decade of the century, told me how Frank Norris came to write *The Pit* as a serial for his paper, and how dependent his family was every week on the miserable pay he received for writing it. The last chapters were written during Norris's wife's illness, while Norris borrowed a few dollars every day from other newspapermen to pay the doctor and buy medication. Theodore Dreiser had to accept every kind of menial job while writing, and I have it from Dreiser's own mouth that he didn't get $200 out of *Sister Carrie* when it was first published, that he had lived on the bounty of his brother, Paul Dresser, the songwriter, who wrote "On the Banks of the Wabash," and that he had to accept a job as foreman of a railroad gang to earn bread and bed after the book was published.

≈

Now that one sees so many newspapermen at the Algonquin and at other high-priced restaurants, one forgets the status of newspapermen before they, too, banded together. The salaries were miserable. Their working conditions were even more miserable than the salaries. With no security whatsoever, they were fired from their jobs without an hour's notice. Driven to desperation and drink by insecurity and humiliation, many of the best men drifted away to other occupations; some to better paying ones, others to less honorable. It is really a miracle that so many of them have emerged as important writers from the newspaper world: Carl Sandburg, Ben Hecht, Sherwood Anderson, Edgar Lee Masters, Franklin P. Adams, Burton Rascoe, to mention but a few of the older ones in Chicago, and Heywood Broun, Alexander Woollcott, George Kaufman, and many more, of New York. Successful writers talk nostalgically about the good old days, but what is really in their minds is their own turbulent youth, colored by old eyes. One should always remember that Harry Armstrong, the composer of "Sweet Adeline," was working in a Boston jewelry store and doing a little boxing and piano-playing on the side to make a living, before his song was published, and that Richard Gerard, who wrote the lyrics, was a postal clerk at the time. The author of "Smiles," Lee S. Roberts, was selling player piano records for a living. The mistake most people make is in thinking that a jewelry salesman who boxed a little and a piano record salesman wrote those songs. The reverse is true. Born songwriters had to "box a little" and sell records because they weren't able to earn a living by their particular gifts.

Another one of the causes of the precarious condition of people in the arts until the first decade of the century was due to lack of communication and difficulty of transportation. Today, when one sees thousands of autos on the streets of New York, one has difficulty in realizing that only yesterday the stone-paved streets clattered under the hooves of horses, and that hansoms, carriages, and buggies were the means by which the "better class" traversed longer distances, while the street cars, which were still horse-drawn, and the elevateds, which went only from south to north and back again, were used by the plain people. There were no telephones in every house, and the streets were badly lighted. In the winter, because there weren't many skyscrapers to act as windbreakers and there weren't many vehicles on the streets, the snow piled up high and slush and snow made walking difficult. The Algonquin, situated as it is on Forty-Fourth Street, was not as accessible as it is today—not if you lived ten blocks away.

~

The people of the theatre were the first to discover in the owner of the Algonquin, Frank Case, a kindred spirit. Some of the best theatres were already located in the vicinity: Belasco's, the Empire, Conried's, the Garrick, Wallack's, and the Criterion were all within walking distance of the hotel. Famous actors and actresses had been in the habit of dropping in for tea at Mrs. Mouquin's Patisserie, only a few steps away from the Algonquin. The Mouquin Patisserie was an adjunct of Mouquin's famous restaurant, and it was lorded over by Madame, a charming Frenchwoman, beloved by all the people of the theatre. I have a suspicion that Frank Case used to drop in there from time to time to meet and to make the acquaintance of stage folk. Without being of the fraternity, he was by nature as close to them as any layman could possibly have been. The truth is that Frank Case was a splendid actor, off-stage, of course, who could turn on charm with the best.

And so, before long, Anna Held, Richard Mansfield, John Drew, E. H. Sothern, and perhaps Lillian Russell and Maude Adams found themselves in tete-a-tete in the lobby of the Algonquin, while Minnie Maddern Fiske and her favorite playwright, Clyde Fitch, were discussing matters of importance across a table in the dining room. Lew Wallace, of *Ben-Hur* fame, and George Ade looked in from time to time. These were probably the first guests of the theatrical world at the Algonquin, and since they were already people of reputation, they, no doubt, attracted others of lesser fame who wanted to be seen in their proximity—when they had the price of a decent meal. To be seen is the first concern of an actor; to be seen with someone famous is a foot in the door to fame.

Around 1910, the hotel was becoming more and more a second home to theatrical folk. Vernon Castle and his wife, Irene, who had created a sensation more because of her bobbed hair than for her dancing, used to drop in and stay for dinner. Occasionally, between tours, they would also stay on for a few days in a suite of the hotel.

The wonderful Cissie Loftus, whose bag of theatrical tricks was fuller and more varied than that of any actress of her day, had her suite in the hotel and her seat in the lobby. Years later, when I saw her in California, an old lady doing imitations of famous women and characterizations of women not so famous, she told me she had often caught something in the attitude or unconscious behavior of people while she sat in the lobby with a cocktail before her. She was also one of the first women to smoke in public. Frank Case, who was opposed to women smoking in public, was so intimidated, he didn't dare ask her to stop. One day, he told her that he had placed a beautiful cigarette case, with cigarettes in it, and an ashtray, in her room. Cissie sailed up to her suite and brought the cigarette case down, to smoke where she wanted to smoke, telling everybody: "Look what Mr. Case gave me. Have one."

Beautiful Laurette Taylor, to whose charms women as well as men succumbed, was an almost permanent guest for breakfast in those early days. I shared several of them with her, her husband, and Clare Sheridan, the English sculptress and writer, a striking beauty, and a very informal lady. La Taylor always occupied the same table and was served by the same waiter, who knew her eating habits so well he never asked what she wanted but served everything unasked. You can't have the same waiter today, every day. They rotate, by order of their union.

Walter Hampden and Richard Bennett would come in, singly or together, and a more contrasting pair was seldom to be seen. And Alla Nazimova and Geraldine Farrar, equally contrasting, were frequent guests, as were Ethel Barrymore and Anna Pavlova.

John Drew liked to hold long conversations with Miss Bush, the young telephone operator, who is still at her post, as young as ever after all these years.

One of the earliest and most devoted Algonquinites was Elsie Janis, perpetually young, perpetually buoyant, and as amusing and entertaining off-stage as on. One always knew when she was around, if only because visitors, bellboys, desk clerks, and telephone operators were laughing at something Elsie Janis just said.

Approaching Mrs. Case, who looked rather depressed one day, Elsie asked what she could do to change her mood.

"Will you laugh if I turn cartwheels right here?" Elsie Janis asked and did.

Later on, La Janis became the favorite of the doughboys of World War I, who voted her their "First Lady of the Land." She never felt that she had wasted her time entertaining them, but only that she had done her duty, within the sphere of her ability, and felt no bitterness towards other actresses who, remaining on home grounds, had reaped a harvest of gold and new fame.

∼

Around 1915, the theatrical world was in the majority among the Algonquinites. Mae Murray, Peggy Wood, and Ruth Chatterton, all as charming today as they were then, are still among the frequent lunch and dinner

Figure 6. Elsie Janis, c. 1922. *Source*: Bain News Service, Library of Congress, Prints and Photographs Division.

guests and often attract more attention than some of the most gorgeously sweatered motion picture actresses of today.

Frank Case used to say: "It's a holiday—look into the dining room and tell me it is not. Where else can you see so many grand women in one room?"

He was the most kissed man I have ever known. Women, young and old, just put up their lips when they saw him, and he responded gallantly.

Then there was Marilyn Miller and Jack Pickford (Mary's brother) whom she had just married, Eugene and Willie Howard, Lenore Ulrich, and laughing, stately Ina Claire, singing as she came down in the elevator and continuing her song to the end while she walked up to the desk for her mail and messages or entered the dining room for her meal.

When Marc Connelly was not at the Round Table with Woollcott, Broun, and Kaufman, he was to be found sitting at a table near the door, beside Margalo Gillmore. I shall never forget the effect she had on me, and thousands of others, in the role of the very young girl in Andreyev's *He Who Gets Slapped*; she was an apparition.

Pauline Lord, Irene Bordoni, Jane Cowl, and, somewhat later, Tallulah Bankhead, touched elbows and nodded to the right and left. I first saw Tallulah when she imitated Jeanne Eagels and Ethel Barrymore, to their faces, in Bob Chandler's studio. She hasn't changed; she never will.

∼

Playwrights and writers discovered the Algonquin somewhat later. Elmer Rice, Robert Sherwood, Ring Lardner, Bob Benchley, Marc Connelly, Sherwood Anderson, Eugene O'Neill, Robert Nathan, Henry J. Forman (the then editor of *Collier's* and the American discoverer of Edgar

Figure 7. Margalo Gillmore, c. 1920. *Source*: Bain News Service, Library of Congress, Prints and Photographs Division.

Wallace), H. L. Mencken, Hendrik van Loon, Sinclair Lewis, and many others were attracted by the atmosphere that had already been created and which they helped make known.

Years ago, when the Provincetown Players banded together to produce modern plays, Broadway sneered at the "amateurs." But the amateurs produced Shaw, Synge, O'Neill, Chekhov, and Tolstoy, and the "amateurs" of the Theatre Guild later on produced Shaw, Molnár, and Pirandello. With only limited funds at their disposition, the "amateurs" had to use imagination and intelligence, which proved to be more effective than the ringing lucre.

When Frank Case took over the Algonquin he was an amateur in the hotel business. His previous occupation as a railroad ticket agent and his brief hotel clerkship wasn't enough to stamp him a professional. However, no professional, weighing the pros and cons, would have taken over the hotel from people so anxious to get rid of it, and for cause. Case sought out the "bohemian" elements not only because of their magnetism, but also, shrewdly, because he knew them to be less critical of the accommodations he had to offer than the average traveling salesman or casual transient, and could be induced to think of the hotel as a second home, with all the usual deficiencies of a home. They rose to the bait and accepted and returned the illusion mirrored before them. Making others believe he had forgotten that he was the owner of the hotel, he often criticized, in their presence, the food and the service in his restaurant and the accommodations the hotel offered.

"I really don't know why people come here. They could get so much better elsewhere. Or couldn't they?" In this way he fended off anticipated recriminations.

Reading the roster of the guests of those days, with names already famous or on the way to fame, no one can doubt that most of them could have found more luxurious quarters; especially since the Algonquin charged first-class rates. It was they, the already famous, and not Frank Case, who added the atmosphere in which they moved to the place. Case was "amateur" enough to encourage them to feel at home. He saw to it that something should appear in the newspapers when Douglas Fairbanks jumped over the tables from one end of the dining room to the other to greet a friend, only to find himself shaking hands with a total stranger. He often deliberately released somewhat unfavorable publicity, in order to deny the "rumor" afterwards. He was a wonderful publicity man. As such he was worth his weight in gold.

Figure 8. Frank Case, c. 1945. *Source*: Photo by Carl Van Vechten, Library of Congress, Prints and Photographs Division.

Case became an author by a slow process of osmosis; by rubbing elbows with authors and journalists, as he had also become somewhat of an actor, a gourmet, a connoisseur of wines, of women, of the arts, and the theatre. He might have become somewhat of a ballet dancer or a painter if enough of them had lived at the hotel for any length of time, just as, by his association with wits he had become a wit. The "osmotic" instinct was highly developed in him. He was, in the best sense of the word, an amateur.

Case didn't look like a hotel-restaurant keeper. Tall, lean, always dressed in the best and latest tailored clothes, well-groomed, elegant, flower in buttonhole, he looked like the twin of a successful illustrator, the second vice-president of a bank, or a state senator.

He had no memory for names. He would stand in the lobby and talk to someone for an hour, then go to the head desk clerk, Mitchell, and ask between his teeth: "Who in heaven's name was I talking to?"

One couldn't imagine him standing over pots and pans, beds and tables. As time went on, he assumed a certain detachment from his business and behaved more like a guest of the hotel than the boniface and owner of it. He acted on the principle that the best host makes the guest feel like the host.

As nimble physically as a tight-rope walker, he developed the same quality mentally; for it was no easy diplomacy to weigh the degree of affability to be shown against the degree of the celebrity to whom he was talking. One couldn't show the same intimacy, say, to John Barrymore, with whom he dined frequently, and the same friendly deference to a less-renowned personality of the stage. Not when Barrymore was around.

In Hollywood, actors, as well as writers, are treated according to the weekly salary they receive, and a producer doesn't show the same degree of affability towards a $3,000-a-week actor as to a $10,000-a-week genius. In Hollywood, $5,000-a-week writers or actors are not yet geniuses and don't sit at the same table with $10,000-a-week men. In New York it was different. It was the personality that often had to be taken into consideration, not the earnings. A keen man despite his apparent blandness, Frank usually reversed the process and called the most famous of his guests by their first names and "mistered" the lesser lights.

Fully aware of the fact that celebrities alone could not fill his hotel and his dining rooms, and that the greater percentage of his out-of-town guests came to the Algonquin because they were eager to bask in the shadow of the famous and to make their acquaintance, he did use his prerogative as a host to introduce some of his guests to his lions, when the occasion presented itself. He did it sparingly when the "star" was in the ascendant, and more frequently when the star had been temporarily eclipsed. No one could have done that more casually, to make both people feel flattered by each other's acquaintance. Yet he had a way with him when an out-of-towner seemed to bore or take up too much time of a famous personality to whom he or she had been introduced. Leaving the person to whom he was talking, he would say to the great one: "You are wanted on the phone."

And the great one would understand, excuse himself, and thereafter avoid the bore like the plague.

~

Case usually came down from his apartment on the tenth floor around one o'clock, when his "luncheonaires" were beginning to assemble in the dining rooms. If the cordon at the Rose Room was up, to hold back the diners until they could be seated by the headwaiter, he would take his place at the end of the line, waiting his turn, and look around to see whom to greet first. Those he hadn't seen in a long time had first call: "Welcome home. You're staying with us, aren't you?"

He had an endless fund of stories and knew exactly what story would amuse whom. A gifted storyteller, he never began a story with "have you heard this one," but would stop telling a story as soon as he noticed the flag was down. Still, he could listen to a story he had heard a dozen times, without flinching or giving the slightest indication that he had heard it before, laugh at the top of his voice and then leave the raconteur to go tell someone else how he had just been told an old story and had pretended it was a new one: "And don't you try to tell me another one. One a day is enough."

He could keep his mouth shut on important matters, but he was a small gossip addict.

Though he had a deep appreciation for the personalities of writers, he didn't feel as comfortable with them as in the company of actors. He wasn't a reading man. He kept himself informed about the latest books of "his" writers, and their success or failure, but he had neither the time nor the disposition to read them, not even those of his favorite crony, Joe Hergesheimer. His eyes always lit up when he saw Hergesheimer, and the author of *Java Head* returned the compliment. "Have you read Joe's latest? Grand, isn't it? What is it about? Please tell me. I expect him in today."

An inveterate first-nighter, Case saw all the plays. Books were a little too much for him, despite the fact that in the course of years, he himself wrote a few. In the midst of his first book, after he had worked on it for months, he broke down one day and confessed to Henry James Forman: "I'd sooner be a dishwasher than make a living writing books. How on earth do you boys do it? One word next to the other, and another next to that one. Good Lord! What a chore! I am dying every morning before I put down a word and am dead at the end of an hour."

D. H. Lawrence appeared one day with a group of admirers. Frank had, of course, heard a lot about Lawrence, his work's nature and subject. Lawrence didn't look at all like the distinguished man of letters that he was. He sat far from the table and leaned forward over it and talked and stroked his beard while he ate. As he continued his meal, the chair moved further and further away from the table.

"Is he really a great writer?" Frank asked. "What on earth does a fellow who looks as he does know about love? Do women love him? What's the matter with them? I don't believe it. He can't talk about love from experience. He must be playing by ear." It was a paraphrase of one

Figure 9. Joe Hergesheimer, c. 1940. *Source*: Library of Congress, Prints and Photographs Division.

of Dorothy Parker's quips about a woman who wrote sexy novels: "She's a virgin. She plays sex by ear."

When his friend assured him of the greatness of Lawrence, Case left the table swearing he was going to buy a Lawrence book and read it "even if it kills me. Just to see what a fellow with such table manners has to say."

He had the same reaction to Gertrude Stein, who lived at the Algonquin while on a lecture tour accompanied by Alice Toklas, her friend and biographer. "A wonderful person. Everybody here likes her. She must be a wonderful person because she has attracted so much attention, even from people who don't understand what she says." Frank confessed to having tried to read one of her books "to be in the swim with all the people who read her without understanding her!"

He must have expressed his frustration a little too loudly, because Gertrude Stein, who had more than one pair of ears, turned around in her chair to look at him with her all-encompassing eyes and gave him the smile one gives a naughty child. Frank blushed and ran out of the dining room, never to be seen again while La Stein was there. He would never admit he had been overheard, but maintained that La Stein had a telepathic sense: "Now, I like that woman, Why on earth did I say that about her? She is a great woman and I am a little, insignificant person! It's not her fault but mine that I don't understand her. She understands me. She certainly does, and forgives me."

When Rabindranath Tagore, the Hindu poet, lived at the Algonquin, Frank was in seventh heaven: "A saint. He looks like a saint. Why should he write books?"

Though he was on friendly terms with Alexander Woollcott, Franklin P. Adams, Joe Mankiewicz, Harold Ross, and the other celebrities who had made the Algonquin's Round Table famous, he seldom sat at the Round Table. When someone uninvited had the temerity to sit there, his face darkened as he watched the reactions of the others. He often took the audacious one aside, after lunch, to tell him that "this is a particular table to which outsiders are not admitted."

∽

Case and the late Leopold Godowsky, the pianist-composer, had an affinity for each other. When Papa Godowsky lunched with his friends, Frank felt free to ask the waiter to bring a chair for him, too. Godowsky, rotund and charming, though friendly to everybody, didn't like intruders, but always welcomed Frank by moving his chair to make room for him. The great pianist never treated him as the owner and host of the hotel, but as a good listener. There was this difference between them: Frank told stories; Godowsky, witticisms, always his own, always on the spur of the moment and apropos. Godowsky enjoyed other people's stories, but never repeated them, and Frank usually carried away at least one piquant remark which he tried to ornament and mold into a story.

On one occasion, Frank was terribly upset, because he didn't know how to handle the situation when Godowsky, with a group of friends and his daughters, had come to lunch after the funeral of his young son. Frank wrung his hands in despair and repeated again and again: "What does one say? What should I say to him in his great sorrow?"

"Nothing," I replied.

"What did you say to him?"

Figure 10. Leopold Godowsky, c. 1916. *Source*: Library of Congress, Prints and Photographs Division.

"I just shook his hand and said nothing."

"Look," he said to me, "all those people at his table. They all say something. What are they saying?"

"Nothing. Hollow words, I am sure." Ultimately, not knowing what to say or do, he approached Godowsky's table, touched the coffee pot, said the coffee was cold, summoned the waiter to bring some hot coffee, and backed away without a word of condolence.

Some weeks later, Godowsky said to me: "That was very considerate and delicate of Mr. Case. How much nicer than that idiot, L . . . , who tried to entertain me with his witticisms."

~

Lois Montross once wrote the following poem about Frank Case:

MR. ALGONQUIN

Mr. Algonquin likes his writers
With pearl gray spats and cigarette lighters
With manuscript cases and bone-rimmed glasses
With authors' agents and theatre passes;
And perfectly groomed with creams and lotions
And we think he has the grandest notions!
Mr. Algonquin couldn't bear it
To have his writers live in a garret;
He wants us fed upon canapes
And filet of sole and rich entrees.
He sees our plays and he reads our stories,
And basks in the sun of rhetorical glories.
He likes us to talk of Capri and Valencia
He really invented intelligentsia.
And whoever buys this hymn to him
Will have to pay a price that's grim,
Or I should never dare enter his place,
And look in Mr. Algonquin's face.

∽

Frank Case had written his first book, which received deserved praise from all sides and attracted attention all over the country—enough attention for former guests at the Algonquin to write from everywhere and ask him to autograph copies for them. It flattered him to the point where he forgot how hard the book had come.

Case was not a man to rest on his laurels. He had made a success of the hotel without knowing much of the hotel business; why couldn't he turn the same trick as an author! Proud of his daughter, Margaret, who had achieved some fame as a witty writer in *Vogue* and the *New Yorker*, and expecting his son, Carroll, also to earn his living in the literary field, he concluded that if they could do it, he could do it too, and immediately embarked upon another book.

If the first one had taken a great deal of his time and energy, the second one sapped him even more. He took long months to fill a few hundred pages of rambling anecdotes, and was often ill and depressed, but he had made up his mind to write another book all by himself and not call upon a ghost writer to do the job or upon his daughter, Margaret, to assist him.

He isolated himself for months in his apartment and then took the manuscript to his country home, but he found that second book a much harder row to plow than the first one. Had it not been for the fact that his managers were working smoothly and that the men in charge of the hotel had had long training and were part and parcel of the atmosphere, really devoted to the hotel, the Algonquin would not have survived the book he wrote about it. His absence was felt by his friends and acquaintances. No one could substitute for him. In the eyes of most people, Frank Case was the Algonquin; the Algonquin was Frank Case. The food was the same. The rooms were the same, yet nothing looked the same while he was away.

The writing of the second book increased his respect for writers. When it was finished and in the hands of a publisher, he confided: "Never again. It has made me old and gray."

And then, whispering, as if it were a secret: "You know, Doug (Fairbanks) has often told me he has written many books under a pseudonym: hot novels and detective stories. I used to believe him. I don't, now. I don't believe he could have written books and had enough energy left to be an actor, producer, manager, business man, and acrobat. It takes too much out of a person. Even Doug couldn't have done it, and then jumped over chairs and tables. He was bragging. It left me a cripple, an old man. I couldn't even be a pleasant host while I was writing. It's a miracle that I am still alive. Can you imagine a writer standing on his head, doing somersaults and backflips? If he writes a page a day, it would exhaust him so he couldn't do any of those things. Look at me." And then, pointing to some of the writers lunching in the restaurant; "Look at them. Do they look like acrobats?"

He admitted to one exception: Hendrik van Loon who, besides being a historian, was so many other things. "But," Frank said, "look at the size of the man. He weighs as much as four people. And how long do you think he will stand the pace?" Frank Case was right. Van Loon didn't stand the pace very long. He died with the best years ahead of him.

~

I remember being caught one afternoon in the lobby of the Algonquin Hotel by an air raid alert during World War II. Frank Case, looking

Figure 11. Hendrik van Loon, c. 1940. *Source*: Library of Congress, Prints and Photographs Division.

worried, said to me: "My God! Should a bomb fall on this place now, half of America's writers and actors would disappear into nothingness." And as the elevator brought down more people from their rooms, he added: "My Lord! Look at that. Jesse Lasky, Charles Laughton, Louis Calhern, Hedy Lamarr, Bob Benchley, Rex Beach!" He loved Rex Beach: "I am sure his stories are wonderful. Strong man stories, aren't they?" It was characteristic of Frank to worry about the fate of writers and actors, though among those crowding the lobby were also prominent lawyers, judges, bankers, and businessmen. The Algonquin may not have been a second home to them, but they were nevertheless old clients.

While the alert lasted, Ben Hecht was in earnest conversation with Gene Fowler, with whom he was writing a play; the sage of Baltimore, H. L. Mencken, who had just arrived, was telling a salty story to Sinclair Lewis, who pretended he had heard it before; and the irrepressible Hendrik van Loon was leaning over author Joe Hergesheimer's chair to show him a caricature he had just drawn of him. And there were others: playwrights Robert Nathan and Ben Burman; Sidney Kingsley, Elmer Harris, Elmer Rice, Russell Crouse, Marc Connelly, and I no longer remember who and how many more of the same caliber.

Hendrik, the most popular historian in the United States, also wrote an occasional novel, illustrated his own books, drew caricatures of his friends, and played the violin and the guitar badly, but on the slightest provocation, or no provocation at all. Strangely enough, he was prouder of his deficiencies than of his qualities. He might have forgiven an unfavorable criticism of one of his books, but if you didn't praise his violin playing and general musicianship, you were in disgrace forever. And maybe this wasn't so strange, after all. Albert Einstein is also proud of his performances on the violin. While playing with Leopold Godowsky at the piano, the musician, irritated by the great mathematician's lack of timing, cried out: "Professor! Can't you count! One, two, three . . . !"

When the all-clear was sounded, the lobby emptied rapidly. Some went out into the street, others were whisked upstairs in the elevators. Frank Case took a long breath. He had experienced a few panicky minutes, but wasn't advising his famous guests to spread out to other hotels and other dining rooms in the neighborhood to avoid the annihilation of American letters and the American stage.

~

Shortly after the Pearl Harbor disaster, the War Department sent me on a lecture tour throughout the army camps. The camps, stretching from New York to the West Coast and inland to the borders of Canada and Mexico, were still mudholes dotted with tents and hastily nailed together barracks. Recruits sloshed through mud, drilled with broomsticks and practiced artillery fire with stovepipes.

Arriving at one of those camp's headquarters one morning, all dirt-caked and bedraggled, I asked to see the commanding officer.

"What about?" the sergeant in the reception room wanted to know.

"Just tell him I'm here," I insisted, repeating my name.

While he was gone, an officer came in. His face was familiar, but I could not place him. Seeing me, he cried out: "A sight for sore eyes!" and pumped my hand vigorously. He was a doctor whom I had seen for many years, lunching at the Algonquin, but with whom I had never exchanged a word. He had sloshed through the mud from the other side of the camp to set eyes on an Algonquinite, after reading my name on the bulletin board.

The C.O. sent word to Lt. Colonel D. F. to entertain me while he was in conference with a visiting general. The colonel, who had written many stories for the *Saturday Evening Post* and was an occasional Algonquinite, took me into his office and sent for coffee. For the next half-hour, he, the doctor, and I reminisced about the porters, bellboys, waiters, headwaiters and their peculiarities, and, of course, Frank Case.

"How is Georges? How is the coffee? How is John? His son is stationed here. And Miss Bush. How is she? Will this war ever end?"

At another camp I ran into Colonel Kenneth Littauer, fiction editor of *Collier's*, who was back in army harness after serving in World War I. Introducing me at lunch to the officers, he said: "The mess here isn't exactly what he is accustomed to eating on Forty-Fourth Street, but war does terrible things to all of us."

∼

Outwardly, the Algonquin has little to distinguish it from a dozen other hotels in New York, but it is a hallmark of the city. What Wall Street is to brokers, Broadway to the theatre, Hollywood to the movies, this hotel is to writers, musicians, actors, and to those who, to breathe, require an atmosphere outside the drabness of the commonplace.

Atmosphere is not something tangible that can be selected in a shop out of a thousand other pieces and placed in the right corner by an interior decorator. It is an elusive something, an aggregate of many things, come into existence slowly, not deliberately, from the very people who need it, so they may function properly. Chairs, rugs, tables, lamps, and draperies are outside trappings. One hears often, too often, interior decorators talk about atmosphere and pretend that they can create it. They cannot; no one can. Atmosphere flows out of an intangible something. Atmosphere is what light is to the lamp, what life is to the body.

There are places in Paris, Rome, London, Madrid, Budapest, Bucharest, Constantinople, Damascus, Cairo, and Jerusalem for which certain people make a beeline as soon as they arrive in these cities. These are not the most modern, not the most luxurious, and certainly not the most expensive hotels and restaurants in the world. Anyone can get a better breakfast anywhere in Paris than at the Deux Maggots, where rickety iron chairs are sown out on the terrace overlooking the Place Saint Gervais.

No one there dunks his croissant in the coffee conscious of the fact that Victor Hugo had breakfasted on that same terrace with Hans Christian Anderson, or that he or she sits before the same table and on the same chair once occupied by Anatole France, Heinrich Heine, Rodin, or Balzac.

You get a meal better served than at the Royal in many places at London, but would van Loon or Sinclair Lewis think of leaving London without at least one dinner at the Royal? The same can be said about the Hungaria in Budapest, the Cina in Rome, the Borda in Constantinople, the Florida in Madrid, and the Eden Hotel in Jerusalem.

Atmosphere has evolved a fraternity and sorority that is beyond race, creed, politics, finances, and the span of an individual life. It is in places where you meet or see or greet with a nod or a handshake someone you had seen the year before; two, three, five thousand miles away, in Damascus, Paris, Budapest, or on New York's Forty-Fourth Street. Someone with whom you have a community of feelings, of spiritual longings, an inexplicable something that binds certain men and women together.

~

My first meeting with William Saroyan took place in Hollywood, at a small gathering in the home of an actor. Saroyan's name had not yet become popular, despite the occasional appearance of his stories in O'Brien's yearly anthology of *The Best American Stories*. There were probably not a half dozen people there who had read his stories. Eventually, we two skipped the party and went out for a bite.

"You fellows are accustomed to great luxury, like the Algonquin," he told me. "I am not. Wait. My time will come," he said, leading me into an eatery. I tried to convince him that there were no gilded, carved ceilings at the Algonquin; that what attracted people there was a certain fraternity of interests, not always literary, musical, theatrical, or political; a need for seeing faces, tortured or joyous, of men and women more or less like themselves. Saroyan, however, was convinced that I said all that to make him not be envious: "Come, come: the place must be beautiful. Everybody talks about it. Dudley Nichols, Thamster Winslow, everybody. It must be beautiful."

Some years later, when he had come to New York to see the curtain rise on his first play, he looked at me triumphantly in the lobby of the hotel and his large, dark, Persian eyes twinkled as he said: "I like it here. It's just as you said. No luxury. But I like it. Mr. Case calls me

Figure 12. William Saroyan, 1940. *Source*: Library of Congress, Prints and Photographs Division.

'Bill.' Wonderful, isn't it? This is my cousin, a great writer, too. He likes it here, same as I do."

Saroyan's uncle in San Francisco, one of the world's great chefs, who has invented dishes Lucullus would have praised to the heavens, once told me, after a copious meal in his place with Melvyn Douglas and Francis Lederer, that he would like to be a chef feeding people worthy of the food: "Like at the Algonquin, for instance."

"Have you ever eaten there?"

"No. But I would like to feed people there."

∽

There were years when the rooms of the Algonquin were so furnished, no seeker of comfort or beauty would have lived in them. Yet, during the

Depression, when all the hotels in the city were practically empty, Case's rooms were half-filled: half-filled in the worst time, and not always on credit. The answer to that situation was not in the price or the quality, but in what that one word, "atmosphere," implies.

The same people come back to the same dining room and sit down at the same table to be served by the same waiters, who had seen them grow older, and whose hair they have seen turn gray from black, white from gray, whose voices they know as well as the waiters know theirs. New people, new faces appear, and when they reappear often, become a part of the whole, integrate themselves in the atmosphere until they, too, are missed when they are away.

If you write a book, you autograph a copy for your waiter, and one for John, Raul, Papa Mitchell, and Miss Bush. If your play is produced, you give them complimentary tickets. If you are a musician, you ask them to come to your concert. And you know when Georges's son got married and when John, who is a magician and entertains you at your table with sleight-of-hand tricks when you look depressed, is worried because his son, fighting in the Pacific, has been wounded.

A new writer who has written a good book, an unknown actor who has given a great performance in a poor play, or an old actor who has given a bad performance in a good play is congratulated or consoled, as the case may be, by someone who ceases to be a stranger from that moment on: "The critics are crazy. I enjoyed it. You were wonderful"; "The critics are wonderful. You were great!"

Burton Rascoe used to come early for lunch and stay late, for the opportunity to air his knowledge of the Greek language with Georges, the headwaiter, a graduate of the University of Athens, and well-versed in other languages and literatures. Georges left the Algonquin some years ago, but many a writer and actor goes to see him in his new job to talk to him, to reminisce, and to keep Georges informed of what is going on in his old bailiwick. He earns a great deal more now than he used to make at the Algonquin, but he is a stranger serving strangers in his new job. He doesn't have the same relation to his present clients as he had with the old ones. No Burton Rascoe to talk Greek to him. No van Loon to ask him the correct pronunciation of "Happy New Year!" in the language of Socrates.

⁓

Figure 13. Burton Rascoe caricature by Gene Markey, 1923. *Source*: Library of Congress, Prints and Photographs Division.

You can recline in the lobby seated on a sofa, without being disturbed by an obsequious waiter trying to sell you a drink you don't want. Other people sit in other corners, alone, or discussing a new book or play with friends.

Horace Liveright, the publisher, with a whole building of magnificently appointed offices at his disposition, loved to discuss the publication of a book by one of his authors in the lobby or in the cocktail lounge. "To avoid interruption," he used to say, but as a matter of fact, talk of books was more appropriate there than elsewhere.

Horace introduced me to the Algonquin while I was still employed by the *New York World*, where I wrote a story a week for the Sunday magazine section. One day my editor, John Cosgrave, asked me to call Liveright for an appointment. Mr. Liveright asked me to meet him at the Algonquin for lunch the next day and invited Cosgrave to join us. We met and talked. Liveright proposed to publish my *New York World* stories in book form. During coffee, Liveright took out his checkbook, filled out a check, and said offhandedly: "It's customary to make an advance against royalties. Here is yours: a thousand dollars." I folded the check and stuck it in my pocket with a nod and a "thank you."

"What?" Liveright exclaimed. "No hurrah? No frantic waving? No tears in the eyes?" Turning to Cosgrave he asked, "Does he get thousand-dollar checks every day?" The truth was that I was speechless. It was the first thousand-dollar check I had held in my hands. My first book, *Crimes of Charity*, since become a classic, had netted me $167. I often take a look at that table and wonder how many others have experienced similar sensations at it. Horace is no more, and there isn't another colorful personality like him in the publishing business.

But great things still do happen in that dining room, to authors, actors, and playwrights. The editors of magazines still take their authors to lunch at the Algonquin. The drama critics meet there to decide which playwright, actor, or director deserves their psalms. Cocktail parties, to fete a new star, are de rigueur there, and nowhere else.

～

You could have told by the laughter you heard whether Dorothy Parker was in the dining room. Her laughter is like one of the sharp, reverberating thunderclaps early in spring, and was generally followed by the laughter of her table companions Edna Ferber, Marc Connelly, and Franklin P. Adams. George S. Kaufman's loudest expression of mirth is a scratch on his unshaven chin. For years now I have tried to catch him laughing: him and Groucho Marx, whom he resembles.

John Barrymore's laughter was a series of short, staccato peals that began with a deep grunt and ended like a clash of cymbals. People talk about his profile, his beautiful speaking voice, his acting. My memory of him is of that animal laughter, that abdominal laughter that was like a loud wind crashing through a primeval forest; an absolutely uninhibited laughter as uninhibited as the man himself.

Van Loon guffawed, always at his own jokes, and would mutter in Dutch, French, or Italian when somebody else told an amusing story. If it was very amusing, he was wont to say: "I would never have expected it from you." He was ready to admit that there were some greater writers and painters than he, but he firmly believed that he was the Prince of

Figure 14. Dorothy Parker, 1933. Courtesy of the Dorothy Parker Society Archives.

Storytellers; and, of course, a musician. He never forgot that. He could be very sarcastic on occasion, but often palliated his most cutting remarks with: "I bear nobody malice, not even myself, and God knows I have good reason for that."

The prize for loud laughter must be handed to Harry Hershfield, who lunches daily at the Round Table in the Oak Room. Harry is the only humorist I know who enjoys his own jokes before, during, and after he tells them. When he is on the radio, you can hear him giggle before he comes up to the mic, and whether or not you laugh, you can hear him laugh in a zigzag of loud giggles. He bounces into the dining room, smiling and shaking hands with the innumerable people he knows, with a mouthful of stories ready before he sits down at the table.

There is a serious side to Harry. He is interested in local, national, and international politics and affairs, but ends a long dissertation with a humorous, apropos story. Jack Alicoate and Lou Nizer are his best audience. Their faces broaden in anticipatory smiles before Harry has begun to tell a story. There is little malice in the stories he tells at the table, but there is a hidden barb in every one. What you hear that same evening on the radio, or at one of the banquets he MCs, is the same story, cleaned up, softened, and the sting gentled. At the table, it is a diamond cut with an axe.

Frank Kingdon has to hear the story to the end before his laughter approves . . . sometimes he admonishes with: "Now, Harry." When he does laugh, everybody in the room stops eating and looks enviously at the Round Table. I shall come back to the Nizer, Kingdon, Alicoate Round Table, also known as the "Soap Box," because of the serious matters discussed around it.

Harry's friends played a trick on him one day. Before he arrived, they conspired not to laugh at any of his stories. As usual, Harry told his first "best" before he sat down. No one laughed. So he launched into a "listen to this one": still his friends looked down at their plates and didn't laugh. Harry turned as pale as a pale man can be. He told a third story—surefire—somewhat to the left of center. Claude Lee, Jack Alicoate, Jesse Lasky, Kingdon, Nizer, and the rest could hardly contain themselves, but kept straight faces. Harry passed a hand over his face and looked through his fingers. It was too much for Nizer, who burst out in loud laughter and confessed the conspiracy.

"You almost gave me heart failure," Hershfield said, and there was no stopping him for two hours.

Robert Nathan, the author of *The Bishop's Wife, One More Spring*, and *Portrait of Jennie*, one of the most subtle stylists writing today, is a good laugher, only he laughs about things nobody else does. The things that strike him as funny don't cause a smile on anyone else's face. A misplaced word, a strange accent, the title of a book, the color of a cigarette holder, make him laugh. His laugh is a one-shot affair, like a sharp cleaver coming down on a hard block. He was the champion swordsman of America at one time and used to dispose of his antagonists with short thrusts. His uncle, the late and lamented Supreme Court Justice Benjamin Nathan Cardozo, had a similar sense of humor and the same kind of laughter.

Tallulah Bankhead leans forward almost across the table, throws her head back, and roars in that inimitable hoarse, deep voice that thunders even when she whispers.

Louis Calhern's laughter is a crackling of high-pitched "oh, oh, ohs"

Figure 15. Robert Nathan. *Source*: Courtesy Robert Nathan Estate.

and "ah, ah, ahs." The moment he stops laughing, his voice deepens. Lou Calhern never talks about his great successes, but always about his failures, and points to them with ironic humility. If anything has gone wrong on the road, or during the out-of-town tryout of a new play of which he is the star, Calhern is the first to tell about it to steal a march on his best friends and critics. Told at an Algonquin table, the tale of the mishap spreads quickly to Broadway, to the newspaper columnists, and the radio and television commentators. By the time the critics are out with their stuff, it's an old tale and doesn't cause a dent in the Calhern armor.

~

Rusty, the Algonquin cat, had the run of the place. Huge, brown, slow-footed, he crossed the floor of the lobby with dignified grace, to curl up

Figure 16. Louis Calhern and Paul Robeson playing baseball in Central Park, 1943. *Source*: Library of Congress, Prints and Photographs Division.

on the seat close to one of the familiars he favored, eventually to follow the select one to the dining room or to the elevator. He knew which guest went to which room. He was a beautiful animal and was as well-known to the habitués as Papa Mitchell, the room clerk, or Miss Bush, the operator. Rusty traveled only on the passenger elevator. When he wanted to visit with the Cases, he got off at the tenth floor. For his afternoon snack, he stopped at the fourth floor, where one of the housemaids fed him his daily portion of liver. Algonquinites temporarily in Hollywood seldom failed to ask of a newcomer: "And Rusty? How is Rusty?"

During the cocktail hour, on a winter afternoon, Case sat on a sofa in the lobby with Rusty curled up in his arms and looked worried. I never was taken in by Frank's worried look. His storytelling technique was to begin a sad story in a humorous way and a rollicking yarn with the mien of an undertaker. He never telegraphed his blows. It was a technique he had acquired from Ring Lardner.

Watching Frank stroke the cat with his thin, nervous hands, I asked: "Anything the matter?"

"I'm worried, really worried," he replied, looking up sadly as he set the cat down gently. "I'm worried about Rusty," he added, his eyes following the feline making his way between sofas and chairs to the elevator.

"Is he sick?"

"No, no. He is as well as can be." Frank, a Christian Scientist, didn't believe in the existence of physical illness.

"Do you know anybody who has a cat just like Rusty? Same color, same markings?" he asked.

"No. But why?"

"Because he is getting old. Cats pass away, too. When he goes to cat heaven, I'll have to replace him with one exactly like him, so people won't notice his disappearance when it happens. I don't want our friends to miss him."

He never admitted that he was physically ill. When Frank's stomach was on the blink, he ate cornflakes soaked in milk, served in a covered dish, as if it were a porterhouse steak. No. He wasn't ill; he ate steaks.

"Worrying about Rusty," he continued, "I am reminded of the trouble I once had with Raymond Hitchcock, a great comedian and a gentleman, but a very peculiar one. You remember him, don't you? You never knew what he'd say or do the next moment. He used to bring all kinds of people up to his rooms, to entertain them late at night, after his performance at the theatre. The day wasn't long enough for him. He loved to see people laugh, to make them laugh. He even brought up a live goat once, to make his friends laugh, and kept it in a clothes closet until we found out." Frank laughed. "I'm laughing now, but it was no laughing matter to get that goat out of his room. Well, you can imagine how the furniture in Hitchy's suite looked.

"Couches sagged, chairs broke down. Carpets withered. He never used an ash tray, but squashed his cigarettes on tables, desks and bedposts. He was a most fastidious man. His gray spats, his blue tie, his cane, his hat and clothes were immaculate. But his rooms! Good Lord!

"While he was away on a tour, I emptied his suite of everything but his trunks and clothes, repainted the walls and refurnished the 'joint' as he called his apartment, from top to bottom. When he returned, I took him up personally to his suite, just to watch the look on his face as he entered the apartment.

Figure 17. Raymond Hitchcock, c. 1915–1920. *Source*: Bain News Service, Library of Congress, Prints and Photographs Division.

"He took one look and cried out in horror: 'This is not my joint! I want my rooms back!' And he wouldn't even spend the night there. We had to dig up the old stuff, even the frayed carpet, before he'd consent to move back into his rooms. After that experience, it took us a year to change everything in it slowly: a chair one week, a sofa the next, a table the month after. We literally stole the things into the room, like thieves. We did the whole thing so gradually, he never realized what had happened. Six months later, everything was ruined. But it was Hitchcock. I loved that man."

~

Neither Frank Case nor Ben Bodne, the new owner of the Algonquin, could have given the hotel what it has, were it not for their flair for the "different," the "unusual," with which they identified themselves. That the owner of a hotel could be host enough to think that his guests would be disagreeably disturbed by Rusty's disappearance, and that he should replace the broken-down furniture piece by piece, worming them in, so to speak, is not the ordinary pattern of behavior of hotel-keepers. Neither the substitution of another Rusty nor the substitution of furniture could have been carried out without the collaboration of a dozen other employees in the hotel. Frank Case was a great host, but he couldn't have functioned without the assistance of all who worked for him and understood and loved the place as well as he did.

When Frank passed away, old Algonquinites wondered what would happen to their favorite hotel. What would the new owners do to and with it? It did need rejuvenation. Would they redecorate it, from top to bottom? Case had reached the stage where he didn't notice how creaky and decrepit some of the chairs and sofas in the lobby were. When his manager or Papa Mitchell attracted his attention to the broken down look of some of the furniture, he soured on them. Many of the unsightly patches on the walls were covered with paintings and caricatures. Some of the rooms were in such a state, they looked as if Hitchcock had just left them.

Frank Case had become more interested in people than in the physical appearance of his hotel; more interested in his reputation as a wit, raconteur, and author than in the furniture of the place. The china was of ages past and the silverware had long ago been worn down by thousands of lips in the dining room and millions of scaldings in the scullery.

The dining rooms continued to be crowded for lunch and dinner, and the rooms were filled to capacity after Case passed away, but many familiar faces disappeared. Old Algonquinites wandered from restaurant to restaurant, trying to find a niche elsewhere. Others just stuck to their workrooms and offices, telling themselves that though they missed the company and the atmosphere of their favorite hotel, they were better off with a sandwich and a glass of milk.

∼

One noon, Harry Hershfield led a smooth-shaven, graying young man to the Oak Room Round Table and presented him: "Ben B. Bodne. The new owner."

"Sit down. Welcome. May we offer you something?" Nizer asked.

"No, thanks. I've just had my lunch. But may I offer you gentlemen anything?" Mr. Bodne inquired, sitting down.

"It's the custom at this table," Jack Alicoate said, sententiously, "to treat a guest and not to have him treat his hosts. This is our table." And before Bodne, who was taken aback, could answer, he continued in the same tone: "Are you a hotelkeeper by profession?"

"No. I'm an oil man from Charleston. Never owned a hotel in my life."

"Then why did you buy this place?"

"Because I liked it. Just because I liked it. It sort of appealed to me," Mr. Bodne said simply, as if he were talking of a painting or a piece of jewelry.

When Bodne left the table, Hershfield remarked: "Boys, everything will be OK. He bought it because he liked the joint. That means you, me, all of us."

"He'll transform it like all hell," somebody opined. "He'll make it look like any of a dozen dining rooms. Watch the interior decorators inching in to make the place more 'cheerful'; to give it character. Watch Mitch replaced by a younger man, Miss Bush by a painted doll, and Raul and John sent away. He'll change everything and everybody." But it didn't happen that way. There was no invasion of "inching" interior decorators. The physical aspect of the Algonquin has been subtly and slowly renewed, but not changed.

The old employees are still in their places, from the basement to the top floor. John is still there. So is Raul, Mitchell, Miss Bush. And if you want breakfast in your room, Nick, who has served room breakfasts for thirty-five years or more, will bring it to you, with a smile, and say "good morning" in Greek. Familiar faces are back. What Frank Case did to Hitchcock's room, Ben Bodne has done to all the rooms of the hotel.

Familiar faces are back. New faces have become familiar ones. The new and the old mingle.

~

Rusty outlived Frank Case by three weeks. A new cat has taken possession of the lobby without exhibiting any inferiority complex because of his famous predecessor. Rusty's death was reported in national obituaries and on the airwaves. A French paper wrote: "Monsieur Rusty, died suddenly at his home in the Algonquin Hotel."

The suite once occupied by Hitchcock is now tenanted by Charles Laughton. Sinclair Lewis's rooms are occupied by Ben Hecht. Douglas Fairbanks's apartment is occupied by his son when he is in town, or by Melvyn Douglas when he is away from his wife, Congresswoman Helen Gahagan Douglas. Alexander Smallens, the famous conductor, occupies the suite Hendrik van Loon used when in town.

Plus ça change, plus c'est la même chose.

~

Leopold Godowsky's wit and sarcasm was the delight of only those at whom it was *not* aimed. Those who were touché, were very touché.

A short man, his feet just about reached the pedals of the piano, and his hands were so small they could hardly encompass an octave. He was a master pianist, but his artistry was not greater than his wit. His tongue lashed out like a rapier. What made his cuts deep was the soft tone of his voice, and the mellowness when the tongue was at its deadliest. To give his stories verisimilitude, he always hung them on some well-known person. He had a few pegs he used constantly.

He was one of the most beloved of men, but years after his death some people are still smarting when his barbs are repeated by musicians in cafés, union halls, and on stage during rehearsals. Toscanini's blunt remarks stun; Godowsky's lacerated. Toscanini's wit is of the sledgehammer type; Godowsky's weapon was a scalpel.

One of the world's famous violinists happened to be in Germany when Hitler came into power. The day the erstwhile paperhanger became the ruler of Germany, our papers were filled with descriptions of the beastly and inhuman wreckage and carnage committed by his storm troopers, celebrating their leader's rise to the top rung of the German nation. Trained as vandals, they wrecked shops and stores, destroyed all opposition papers and publications, broke into the offices of labor unions, beating up and crippling whoever they found there, and wound up the orgy by invading Jewish homes and establishments to rape and murder to their hearts' content. Thousands of Berlin Jews were dragged by the heels through the gutters to be thrown into Gestapo cellars in which they disappeared unless ransomed by their friends, or if they agreed to sign over their wealth to this or that Gauleiter. And even then, as a parting humiliation, they were paraded through the streets with humiliating placards hung from their necks, on which the grossest insults to themselves were lettered. Famous Jewish authors, artists, scientists, their wives and daughters were made to clean the streets. Many American papers carried photographs showing Jews compelled to clean the latrines with their tongues, under the supervision of whip-carrying storm troopers, while the populace looked on and laughed at a spectacle that would have been considered barbarous in the Middle Ages.

That world-famous violinist left Berlin three weeks after the beginning of that orgy. When he landed in New York, reporters interviewed him and expected a visual description of the savagery that had outraged the world. For reasons best known to the man, he denied that he had witnessed any indecency, any rioting.

"But there were pogroms?" one newspaperman asked. "You have no doubt witnessed them."

"I didn't see anything like a pogrom. Some of the boys got a little boisterous and maybe broke a few windows. No worse than when the American Legion is in town."

"But we've seen photographs of wrecked stores owned by Jews and the wrecked offices of newspapers and union offices and photos of women being beaten and maltreated on the streets of Berlin and Munich," another reporter prompted.

Our violinist shook his head: "Propaganda. Just anti-German propaganda. I was born in Germany. I know my Germans. They are a civilized people, incapable of such or any other kind of barbarism. It's just communistic propaganda."

"But Mr. ——, how can a Jew who has seen these things with his own eyes deny that they have taken place?" asked a reporter from a Yiddish paper.

"I, a Jew?" the violinist cried. "I haven't a drop of Jewish blood in me." And he scurried away.

"What made you say he is a Jew?" one of the reporters asked the Jewish newspaperman.

"Because I know he is."

A week later, Godowsky landed in New York from a trip to Austria, where he had gone to settle his affairs prior to taking up permanent residency in the United States. Reporters met him at the Algonquin and questioned him about Germany. "Yes, I was in Germany. I had to pass through Hitler's country to come back here. Ah," Godowsky cried, "that

I should have lived to see such things. It was unimaginable! The world has never seen such unspeakable behavior. It made me feel ashamed to be a human being."

A reporter asked: "Do you know Mr. ———?"

"Of course. I've known him since he was a boy. I knew his father and mother. What about him?" Godowsky asked, alarmed.

"He was in Germany the day Hitler and his gang took over. He came back to New York a week ago. We asked him to tell us what he had seen. He told us that nothing extraordinary had happened. No worse than when a Legion convention is held in a town. He said all reports to the contrary were anti-German propaganda; that he hadn't seen any maltreatment of Jews in the streets."

"He said that!" exclaimed Godowsky. "How could he find it in his heart to defend the storm troopers? He, a Jew!"

"But," said a reporter, "he said he didn't have a drop of Jewish blood in him."

"Ah!" Godowsky exclaimed, showing great anxiety. "Poor man! When did he have such a terrible hemorrhage?"

The effect was terrific. The story spread in many variations, and the violinist couldn't show his face for months and played to empty halls all season.

∾

Mrs. Case was an unobtrusive person. Intimates called her Bertha. She had none of the qualities of the host possessed by her husband. She was seldom seen in the lobby of the hotel and only rarely in the dining rooms, when she lunched or supped with Frank or with some friends. She was so little noticed by the habitués of the hotel that she was gravely ill for months before anybody missed her, and then only after Case had expressed his anxiety. Frank followed her into the beyond a year later.

∾

Frank Case was an amateur when he took over the Algonquin. Professional hotel men were certain he would fail. He didn't, and after forty years of ownership, during which many hotels owned by professionals in the neighborhood went down one after the other, he left behind an establishment that had become an institution, a landmark, not only of the city, but of the whole country, while it had made him a sizable fortune.

The new owner, Ben B. Bodne, also came to the hotel as an amateur. The difference between the two men is that Frank took over the place with hardly any money, while the new owner, after paying a sizable amount for the property, still had enough left to carry on without having to count pennies.

Ben B. Bodne was born of immigrant parents and was raised in Charleston where, while still going to school, he had to contribute to the family exchequer by selling newspapers on the street. Someday, someone will write the history of all the successful men in America who started out life as newsboys. It would make interesting reading, particularly to people in other countries, and teach them how, at an early age, Americans make their apprenticeship in business to teach them self-reliance. I would personally pay the Marshall Plan administrators to print such a book, in several languages, and distribute a dozen million copies, gratis.

There was an old saying in our country that wealth passes so rapidly from one set of hands to another that there was only one generation between shirtsleeves and suits. This is no longer true. The old fortunes are no longer concentrated in the families whose founders had accumulated them. The rising generations must create new wealth by their industry, audacity, ingenuity, and spirit of adventure.

How Ben Bodne made his way from the penny-a-paper business into big affairs that enabled him to accumulate a sizable fortune before he was forty-five is a story to be told elsewhere, but it is interesting to note what made him determined to become the owner of the Algonquin.

Bodne married when he was about twenty-five and the young couple went to New York on their honeymoon. It was the first time he was really away from business. For years he hadn't had a day off: one business activity had led to another and he had to spend weeks on the road, selling or organizing a sales force. He had taken his first bite in the oil business just before he got married and had made what he considered then a great profit out of that first venture. What he had made until then came from comparatively small affairs, all kinds of ventures; but he risked all he had in one big transaction and went through hell before he could count the profits.

"I don't know why, when we arrived in New York, we went to the Algonquin. It was, I think, due to my wife, who is much more of a reader

Figure 18. Harpo Marx, Ben Bodne, and Bodne's wife, Mary, 1961. *Source*: Courtesy Michael Colby.

of books and magazines than I am and who had read about the hotel and the people who lived there. Anyhow, there we were, on our honeymoon; young, eager, and with all the money we could spend.

"Like all out-of-towners, we were anxious to see as many plays as possible in the few weeks we had allotted ourselves. I have always liked the theatre and seldom missed a play when it came to our town. As a matter of fact, I have always liked all kinds of spectacles; the cinema, too, and sports of all kinds. Baseball, basketball, box matches; they were my relaxations, and Mrs. Bodne liked them, too.

"Back at the hotel the first night, we noticed some of the actors we had seen on the stage coming into the lobby. It was all so different from any hotel I had ever been to. Everybody seemed to be as easy of mind as in their own homes. There was a mellowness and a quietness that greatly appealed to both my wife and me. Mitchell was at the desk, as now. Miss Bush was at the switchboard. John served us. So, instead of going up to our room, we sat in the lobby quite a while and looked around.

"We came down the next morning and sat in the lobby after breakfast, just watching people, seeing how congenial they were. No one seemed to hurry. Nobody pressed anything on you. No doubt many of the people had cares and responsibilities, but they didn't seem to carry them on their minds as did the people I had met in other hotels. They talked and laughed during breakfast, or chatted with the waiters and the clerks. We lounged comfortably and lunched and dined, served by a waiter who acted as if he had known us a long time. As a matter of fact, John, the present headwaiter in the Rose Room, was the waiter who served us then. He was kind, affable, when we inquired who this one was, who that one was, and told us where this one was acting and in what play, and what book that lady with the big hat had written.

"When he thought we looked lonely, he came over to our table and amused us with his sleight-of-hand tricks, Just as he does today.

"Within a few days, we felt that we, too, were of the crowd, and wondered whether someone wasn't asking John who we were. We were neither actors nor writers, but seeing them so close and finding them so friendly, it made us feel that we, too, belonged. We were on the other side of the footlights, but we belonged.

"When I began to think about returning home, to business, to the hustle and bustle, it was without much pleasure. So, one evening, after we had met a few of the celebrities, casually, without trying too hard to meet them, I said to my wife: 'That's the kind of business I'd like to be in. That's the kind of people I'd like to meet; to talk with, to dine with. Well, we'll own this place someday.'

"I don't know what made me say it. But my wife thought it would be wonderful; that she would like nothing better."

It is characteristic of a businessman to want to own the place in which he feels at home. He doesn't really enjoy a place until it is his. When the Bodnes went back to Charleston and he returned to his activities more vigorously than ever, fighting for every dollar with men who were as intent to get it from him as he was to get it from them, his business interests became more diversified. When his financial condition became more secure and he was cutting a figure in the community where he had started as a newsboy, the world was his oyster.

He should have been content with what he had, but every once in a while, during a lull or during a train trip, his mind would revert to the Algonquin, to the peace and mellowness he and his wife had experienced there, and he would repeat to himself that someday he would own the place. Hotels, in general, held no attraction for him. As a matter of fact, he didn't like them. Only the one hotel obsessed him. Although he ventured into many different kinds of business, acquiring the know-how the hard way, through losses and heartaches, he never invested his money in hotels.

The oil business held his attention and he was making big money. Everybody considered him a happy man. Measured by the size of his yearly earnings and his bank books, he was a successful man. Few who had started with so little had become so successful at his age, and he was occasionally called upon to speak at different business organizations and asked to tell the secret of his success: "I told them a lot of things: the usual stuff about hard work and only taking considered risks; of giving a chance to good men in my organization; of economy and of not dabbling in things I knew nothing about.

"I told them that, but deep down in my heart I knew I wanted to go into a business I knew nothing about: that I wanted to own and run that hotel to which I had taken my wife on our honeymoon. You may say it was a crazy idea. And perhaps it was. But as the years went by, that idea recurred frequently in the midst of discussions and haggling about affairs as remote from the ownership of a hotel as one could possibly imagine.

"I never spoke about it to anybody, but mentioned it to my wife occasionally. She never discouraged me, never told me not to waste myself on idle dreams. Deep down in herself, she, too, had the same dream. Whenever she saw the Algonquin mentioned in a paper or magazine, she'd clip the item and show it to me: 'Here is something about your Algonquin.'

'My Algonquin!'

'Our Algonquin.'

"I was heartbroken when, during one of my trips to New York, I couldn't get a room there. I took a room at a hotel across the way, but I had my meals in the Rose Room. John, the waiter, whose hair had turned somewhat gray, recognized me and sat me at the same table my wife and I had sat at some years before. It flattered me to be recognized. John has the most remarkable memory I have ever encountered.

He sees a person once and he is photographed on John's mind. Years later he will remember what so-and-so had for lunch and how he likes his eggs. I was pleased to see some of the same faces I had seen when I was there with my wife.

"Some waiters and hotel captains have long memories for faces, and they remember particularly the faces of people who tip them well. Waiters and clerks in hotels all over the country had called me by name after not seeing me for a year or two, but John's gesture struck a particularly warm chord in me. I looked around and saw many familiar people, some of them were even sitting at the self-same tables. How different it was from the hotels in large cities that I frequented during my business trips where I seldom saw the same face twice.

"As I left the dining room, Mr. Case, to whom I had been introduced, came over and said: 'Are you staying with us?'

"It was as if he, too, remembered us. When I told him that I was not, he acted really sorry; as if he were guilty because they had no room for me.

"You know, in the business world we believe that actors, artists, writers, are peculiar people; that it's best to have no truck with the bunch. But I was drawn to them.

"'You should have made a reservation. Next time let me know,' Frank Case said.

"We stood and talked for a while. He inquired about my wife, inquired what business I was in, and then asked: 'What made you come here in preference to any other place, to begin with?'

"'Because I like it here.'

"'The best reason in the world,' he said. 'the best I've heard yet. Come, let's have a drink on that.'

"We went to the bar, drank and talked. He wanted to know how business was, and I told him. Maybe I bragged a little. 'How would you like to be in the oil business?' I asked him. 'There is money in it. More than in the hotel business.' Mr. Case laughed. 'This is the business I like: the people I like. I'd rather be here than be the King of Siam.'

"I didn't tell him 'so would I,' but that's what I felt. When I returned home, I repeated that conversation to my wife. It was more interesting to me than the talk with businessmen I had had. She asked whom I had seen. I knew only a few names, but described some of the people we had both seen there. She remembered. Every time we had seen those names mentioned in a newspaper or had seen their pictures, we had felt as though they were old friends.

"'Next time I'll go with you, she said. 'I should have gone to New York with you this time, too.'"

More years went by and Ben Bodne, the erstwhile newspaper boy, became a wealthy man. One doesn't become wealthy using butterfingers, and I can well imagine the rough and tumble this man went through in a rough and tumble crowd whose early apprenticeship in business was not different from his. I have read too many tales about oil men not to have a fair idea about the struggles involved in a business in which men either make millions in a single deal or are broken, to rise again out of nothing and begin a second and third and fourth fortune until they drop from sheer weariness. Everything connected with oil is a gamble. The theatrical world is still talking about the millionaire oil man who bought a theatre on Broadway, produced a play he liked, and charged no admission for more than a year. Then, in a single day, he lost all his fortune, closed the theatre, and went back west to make another fortune. When asked why he had produced that play on which he had spent millions, he replied: "I liked the play, I liked the actors, and I liked the people who came to the theatre. I couldn't have had more fun for my money in anything else."

Meanwhile, Ben Bodne acquired a family and was intent on giving his daughters a better beginning in life than he had had. As usual, he drew a number of people from his family and his wife's family into his organization and assisted them to make their fortunes and their own way in life. But again and again the thought of owning the Algonquin came back. To become a part of it, he had to own that place. In moments of relaxation, he planned what he would do with it; how he would improve certain facilities, and discussed these matters with his wife.

I know of some families where the map of the world is studied on winter nights, and plans are made, never to be realized, for long trips, by train, boat, and air. We did that in my parents' home in Romania. We had more maps than we could study. An uncle who sent us a large globe of the world became our favorite. When the winter winds were at their worst and the wolves howled beneath our windows, we leaned over maps and dreamed of ourselves in warm lands.

On their third visit to New York, the Bodnes brought their young children with them; but this time they had wired the Algonquin for reservations. They spent a week in the big city. Mrs. Bodne visited some of her family in New York, but went to the theatre nightly. Mr. Bodne frequently remained in the lobby, looking around, watching what was going on, talking to bellboys, clerks, elevator boys, not with any definite intention: just out of curiosity and to keep his dream going. He lunched in the Rose Room because of John, the waiter, and because he liked to watch the goings-on at the Round Table, to listen to Woollcott's rollicking laughter and to Heywood Broun's guffaws.

On this visit, he discovered that celebrities were not at all difficult to approach; that if one didn't elbow oneself into their presence, they were rather keen to meet people in other fields of endeavor than their own. He even cocktailed with some of them, and Hitchcock, then at the height of his fame, spent an hour with him, telling stories of the road, and wound up inviting him to his room. "What a room! It looked as if a hurricane had swept through it!"

Later, when Hitchcock appeared in Charleston on a tour, they were old friends when Bodne met him backstage. "Hello Ben!"

"That did it. The next day I was tempted to write a letter to Frank Case and ask whether his hotel was for sale. But I didn't: not because I was afraid he would name some outrageous figure, but because I was afraid he would reply that it was not for sale at any price. I remembered only too well what he had told me: that he'd rather have that hotel than be the King of Siam. Thinking about it, I couldn't blame him. Why should he want to sell it? He made a good living, liked it no less than I did, probably more, since he knew it much better and knew so many of its people. But I couldn't help thinking about the place.

"Years passed by. My daughters grew up.

"Then, one day, my wife called to tell me that she had just read that Frank Case had died. It was rather a harsh blow of fate that a man not too old should die when he was so happy to live the way he had lived. But one man's loss can be another man's gain. I finished my business in New Orleans and headed for New York to find out in whose hands the estate was." The estate was administered by a bank, to whom it was left in trust for the Case children. The trustees were running the hotel without any drastic changes. The Case children had no inclination to carry on the business themselves and were anxious to liquidate it as speedily and profitably as possible.

The Algonquin was for sale. Many professional hotelkeepers had an eye on it, but the price they offered was below what the trustees considered a fair value. When our amateur came along, those who had previously shown interest became indifferent. They learned that while Bodne was a successful oil man, he knew nothing about the hotel-restaurant business: so, they figured, they would let him buy it and buy it back from him six months later for less than half the price he had paid.

The oil man, who had learned a few tricks himself in the oil business, knew what they were up to. The purchase of the Algonquin became an obsession. He was being provoked. He thought of all the deals he had made, sitting across a table. The shrewdest oil men hadn't been able to get the best of him; professional hotel men couldn't do it either. When it became known in the hotel field that the oil man wanted to buy a hotel, he was besieged by many brokers who offered him some of the most renowned hotels in the city. He went to look them over and took his wife and daughters along. When the Algonquin transaction didn't run smoothly and he expressed himself willing to buy another hotel in New York, the family was up in arms. It was the Algonquin or nothing: "We didn't come to New York to buy a hotel, any hotel!"

That was three years ago. He still owns the Algonquin, liking it more than ever despite the vicissitudes of running a hotel without previous experience. He has had to learn the hard way. He has learned. He has practically cut himself off from all other business and interests and is wrapped up more and more in a dream represented by stones, bricks, ovens, pots, beds, sofas, chairs, carpets, and people, the kind of people he likes to be with under one and the same roof. The kind of people whose company he likes. Ward Moorehouse, Alexander Smallens, Arthur Tracy, Charles Laughton, Louis Nizer, Morris Ernst, Dr. Frank Kingdon, and many others.

Says the new owner of the Algonquin: "I don't know what it is, but it's got me. When I am away on other business, I just can't wait to get back. The friends I have made here are so different from my other friends. It has changed my outlook. I am living in a new kind of a world and I like it."

Bodne made some faux pas before he learned his way around. One morning the newspapers carried the information that Ben B. Bodne, the former oil man and present owner of the Algonquin, was heading a sports organization that was about to launch the Tournament of Champions. Every man has a right to engage in whatever business he likes or finds profitable, but when the dining rooms and lobby began to be filled with broken noses, cauliflower ears, and the "dese" and "dose" gentry, there were many, many raised eyebrows.

Bodne, who throws himself wholeheartedly into whatever he does, was so busy with fight managers, publicity men, sportswriters, and others on the periphery of the ring, he didn't notice or realize that certain things don't mix; that he was destroying the very atmosphere that had attracted him. When he did realize it, after friends pointed that out to him, he was too deeply involved to extricate himself on the spot from the Tournament of Champions.

The first match between Rocky Graziano and Tony Zale took place in Jersey City. Zale knocked out his opponent in the sixth round. Ben was at the ringside; his family was at home. When he returned home, his young daughter, Barbara, met him, crying. She had heard over the radio that Graziano had been seriously injured and might not recover. "Is that the kind of business my papa is in? A business in which people get killed?" she stormed. That was the end. Bodne withdrew without hesitation. Did he "drop" some money in the venture? "I would have got out of it anyhow, because of the kind of people one comes in contact with in such a business. Nice people, some of them, but . . ."

~

As an Algonquinite, I had often marveled at the degree of diplomacy needed to keep its denizens satisfied and at peace. An author is disturbed by the clicking of a typewriter in an adjoining suite. While in the throes of inspiration, they don't reflect on the fact that they are disturbing others, too. Instead, they pull their hair out while they stamp furiously about the room. And if they stop to meditate, the other typewriter is going at full speed and so, instead of meditating, their mind drifts and begins to speculate on what the other one is doing. If they know the other's work, they wonder whether they are writing a sequel to the last novel or starting out on something different. Meanwhile, the other author is banging away.

It is unethical to ask another one what he is working on. Only non-professionals ask each other "What are you writing now?" The question is as silly as asking an inventor "What are you inventing now?" Every story, every book, every play, is a new invention. If two authors, living in adjoining rooms, happen to lunch at the same table, they just stare at each other, trying to fathom the other's thoughts; not because either one is jealous, but because they are mutually disturbed by the pounding of their respective typewriters.

Some authors maintain a good disposition while working. Others are irascible and most unreasonable and frequently angry at the whole world. All work is conceived in hope and carried out in doubt. No author can foretell whether he will be able to carry through what he has started; whether he will succeed in transferring his thoughts to paper in such a way that the readers will get what he means to say. This is why writers are disturbed so easily by the noise of other writer's typewriters . . . why they are disturbed, period.

The remedy that suggests itself would be for the management to move one of the authors to another room, but that is more easily said than done. Not only because each one of them is accustomed to their own room, which they had rearranged to suit themselves, but also because each one may have a kind of superstition about their diggings. They have written their best novel there and won't be budged until they have finished what they have on hand. Some have beautiful studios in their own homes, but can't work in them. Some people are superstitious about one thing, others about another: one about a cat passing to the right, another about an electric bulb blowing out at the wrong time, but most writers prefer to work in a room they have worked in before at the same table, sitting on the same sagging chair.

~

An actor rehearsing his latest part in a play is annoyed by the singing he hears coming from somewhere on the same floor, or by the thumping of a piano overhead. And he, too, may be upset by the click of a nearby typewriter. Actors don't have too high an opinion of writers and vice versa: their opinions of each other are best left unmentioned. It is quite possible that the voice that disturbs him is his favorite musical comedy star, to whom he sends flowers every so often, and whom he takes out to supper. But he finds it difficult to concentrate on *Macbeth* while the lilt of a new tune or the trilling of scales assaults his ear again and again. I have yet to meet a dramatic actor who likes music. They do like sopranos and altos, but music . . .

The late Arthur Byron, one of the most distinguished actors, was a very conscientious artist. He not only rehearsed new plays, of which he was the star, but also rehearsed all the other parts of his immense repertoire, to keep his memory in shape. "I never want to forget anything I ever learned. Or, rather, I want to remember everything I have had to learn," he once told me. He never let himself go stale, and kept on rehearsing and improving the roles he was momentarily engaged in and improving the parts he had played years ago. He wasn't a man of moods; he was a perfectionist.

Byron rushed down to the lobby one day, protesting loudly about the typing in the room next to his. "It's been going on all night. I couldn't

Figure 19. Arthur Byron, c. 1920. *Source*: Bain News Service, Library of Congress, Prints and Photographs Division.

sleep. It's noon now and he hasn't stopped. I'm going crazy. Doesn't the fellow ever sleep? He bangs away on the keyboard as if it were a machine gun." Now Mr. Byron was a permanent guest of the hotel, and everybody would have liked to do everything possible to keep him satisfied. He rarely complained about anything, chiefly because he was always absorbed in his own work and had no ears for anybody else's.

When he finished his tirade, Frank Case, who had listened patiently, asked: "But Arthur, do you know who the man next to you is?"

"I don't know and I don't care," Byron cried.

"Perhaps if you did know, you would care."

"Who in God's name is he?" the irate actor asked. When he was told who the man was, he threw his hands up in the air. "Oh my God. It's the author of my play, trying to fix the second act as I asked him to. Don't ever tell him I complained. And don't stop the poor fellow. He must be dead tired by now."

~

Ben Hecht—who has a magnificent home on the Pacific where he has built a special studio to which he can retire and work, and another home in Nyack where he has built a duplicate of the studio in California, overlooking the Hudson—often comes to the Algonquin to finish a play or a scenario. The walls of his suite have to be a certain shade, and he insists on certain pieces of furniture. He works in a rhythm all his own, surrounded by a number of gadgets and playthings, not always the same. The last time I visited him, he had rigged up a target at the far end of the room and was practicing with an air rifle, hour after hour while his secretary sat quietly, waiting for his dictation. He would spend hours popping away with his air rifle and was jubilant when he hit the bull's eye.

Figure 20. Ben Hecht, c. 1919. *Source*: Culver Pictures, Library of Congress, Prints and Photographs Division.

At other times, he walks about the room playing his violin, and although it's a good violin, he is not a very good player. He has been playing it for decades and has trained his fingers diligently in all the errors he acquired from his first teacher forty years ago. It is not unusual for him to spend several days in his room without going out at all; to have his meals sent up and to communicate with his family by phone to Nyack or California. Then, suddenly, he drops the rifle or the violin, and pounds away at the typewriter for hours on end, while his secretary sits and waits.

At work, he gives the impression that the typewriter is a racehorse he is riding to the post. One may quibble about him being a great writer, which he is, but no one can quibble about him being the fastest writer, once he gets started. He has, sometimes, written a whole novel in a day, dictating to two stenographers in relays and typing himself while they transcribed his dictation. It is no secret that he wrote the script of many a movie on which he was paid fabulous sums within a few days. At other times he starts something with his usual fury, goes out for coffee in the middle of a page, and casually takes a train to Nyack or flies to California. The management knows he is gone when they receive a telegram from him or are told by his secretary, who comes to gather the unfinished work, his favorite typewriter, and leaves on the next plane to California.

Ben, who can be the sweetest of men, can also have his tantrums and scream at the top of his lungs when somebody interrupts him. He won't even let the chambermaid clean his room when he is at the typewriter. Later, he inquires who it was he offended and apologizes profusely. He can be as profuse in his apologies as in his profanity. For sheer vigor and color of verbiage, he is as magnificent when he curses as when he apologizes.

∿

Sinclair Lewis, too, comes to the Algonquin to finish his novels. He goes home to Minnesota, stays for a few days, leaves for California or Europe, and comes back to continue from the middle of the page stuck in the typewriter.

Some of his old cronies are no more. He used to love to surround himself with them. When they didn't come to his room, he would go to theirs, forever telling stories, often acting out parts, and at the drop of a hat, ready with his great impersonation of a YMCA secretary, one of the most hilarious bits I have ever heard. When he is absorbed in his work, he walks about like one not of this world and often doesn't recognize his oldest friends nor remember their names.

Mencken, van Loon, and George Jean Nathan staged many a party at which Sinclair Lewis was the chief performer. When in the right mood, he is a whole circus by himself! He should have been an actor. As a matter of fact, he is.

At the end of his work, he seems invigorated, gayer, and ready to have some fun. Any excuse to interrupt work before the last few pages are done is welcome. This may go on for months; with cocktail parties often beginning at breakfast and ending long after midnight. Then, suddenly, the doors are closed. He is incommunicado and won't even answer a telephone call. Miss Bush knows. After the work is in the hands of a publisher, a reaction sets in and Lewis becomes subdued and quiet, comes down to the lobby, lighting one cigarette after another, goes to his favorite table to sit alone in so detached a manner that not even his best friends go over to talk to him. From then on, you watch the publisher's announcement for the title of his forthcoming book. No one ever knows the contents until it is published.

Some time ago, the literary editor of an out-of-town paper came to New York to interview him. She happened to come when Lewis had cut himself off from the world. The literary editor waited patiently and came to the Algonquin every day to inquire whether the great man was approachable that day. After many days, Frank Case told her he thought it could be done that day. Even as he spoke, Lewis came down. The three of them chatted for a while; then the lady approached the elevator and waited expectantly for someone to come down.

After Sinclair left Case to return to his room, she approached Case: "Do you think he'll come down?"

"Who?"

"Mr. Lewis."

"But you've just been talking to him."

"My God!" the lady cried. "Was that Sinclair Lewis?"

And her knees sagged at the thought of the opportunity she had missed. How could she approach him again and tell him she hadn't known who he was while she was talking to him? Eventually she went home without the interview, but wrote one anyhow. Had she had any insight, she would have known that Lewis would have laughed aloud had she confessed to him.

~

There are quite a number of people who like to perform in public. One shouldn't call them exhibitionists because of this alone. Certain people find a kind of isolation when there are other people about. Quite a number of great European writers have done a considerable amount of their work on café terraces. The great short story writer Peter Altenberg used to appear every morning at the Bristol Café in Vienna, where he had once been a waiter, with his briefcase filled with papers and books, and would settle down at one of the tables for the day.

When asked why he worked in public, he replied: "My mother said I was lazy. Soon every one of our relatives took up the cry. I want every one of them to see that I work and that my stories don't grow on trees."

Arthur Schnitzler is supposed to have written his plays in a little café. Strindberg worked best in a beer garden, especially on Sunday, when there was much drinking around him. Ferenc Molnár, the Hungarian playwright, has done most of his work in one of the cafés in Budapest where a certain table was reserved for him. His working hours were somewhere between midnight and six a.m. In a recent interview he confessed that though he has been in New York for many years, he has not yet discovered the right kind of café in which to work. He comes to the Algonquin often, but hasn't yet brought his pencils with him. Maurice Maeterlinck wrote his last stories in the Oak Room, while breakfasting.

Jean-Paul Sartre, the existentialist, has until recently written his books and plays in a café in Paris. To emulate him, all the other existentialists did their work in the same place, so that the café often looked like an improvised office with so many clerks pegging away at their documents. The great French poet Verlaine wrote some of his most lyrical verses at the Café Procope, on the left bank. Rimbaud's favorite workshop was a hallway on the Rue de Rivoli. When driven away by the janitor, he would hide himself under one of the bridges across the Seine.

It would be generalizing to call all these people exhibitionists, but it is disconcerting to see young men and women in the lobby of a hotel, pounding away at a portable typewriter as if their lives depended upon it. No doubt there are some exhibitionists among them. One sees them occasionally in the lobby of the Algonquin. Some are real writers; others do it to attract attention. There is no telling who is what.

~

Some years ago, I employed a male secretary of whose work I had little reason to complain.

But he was a peculiar fellow. A Swedenborgian and the son of a Swedenborgian minister, he had certain religious scruples that bordered on mania. One was that a man had to own his own working tools and so, despite the fact that there was a typewriter in my suite, he would arrive every morning with his portable slung over his shoulder and do all his typing with the machine on his knees.

He lived in New Jersey and his train was occasionally late and the ferry across the Hudson was also not always on time. When Eddie sat down with his typewriter, he would look at his watch and jot down the time on a piece of paper. At the end of every day he presented his bill and demanded his pay, in cash: if he had been seven minutes late, he would deduct it from his pay. He would never admit to himself that he was hired by the day or week. According to his concept, he was no wage slave, was free to leave at any time, and worked by the hour, or the minute, so as not to enslave himself.

He had worked regularly for me for years, yet every evening he asked the same question: "Will you need me tomorrow?" He had to feel he was coming to work not only for pay, but because he was needed. One day, Eddie didn't ask the question and I paid no attention. There was no Eddie the next morning. I expected him, but as the hours went by and he didn't appear, I concluded he was not feeling well.

Eddie frequently went on long fasts, sometimes a week, sometimes two weeks or longer.

At such times he would bring a bottle of water sweetened with honey and sip at it from time to time. He had just been on a long fast, and I had attracted his attention that afternoon to the fact that his hearing had been affected by the fast.

At lunch time, when I went down to the lobby, there was Eddie, pecking away at the typewriter on his knees. When I asked him why he hadn't come up, he answered that he was giving himself a month. The money he had saved during the fast was enough to keep him going that long. When I asked why he hadn't informed me the day before, he replied that he didn't think it necessary; he wasn't my slave, that I didn't need him, or want him, because I had not asked the question as to whether he was to come the following day. "Had you wanted me to come, you would have asked: 'Are you coming?'"

For a month I saw Eddie in the lobby, typing, completely oblivious of his surroundings. At the end of the month, he knocked at my door and asked: "Do you need me?" He had, meanwhile, written a book against vivisection, which was later published and created quite a sensation among people interested in that disputed theory.

Six months later, Eddie went on another fast of thirty days, lost some thirty pounds, and looked like a skeleton. His hearing became quite bad. He again left me suddenly to write another book in the lobby of the Algonquin; this time about vegetarianism.

When I asked him why he came from New Jersey every day to sit in the lobby of the Algonquin, when he could work just as well at home, he looked at me fixedly for a few moments and then said: "What right have you to ask such questions?" He never again came back to work for me. He still writes an occasional book, typing it at some other hotel.

It is lighthearted to dismiss people with such vagaries as freaks. Every normal human being has their own peculiarity. In artists, in intellectuals, those peculiarities are more accentuated, either because they are under observation, in the glare of publicity, or because they are not repressed. Psychoanalysts have reached the conclusion that nothing worse could be done to a creative artist than to analyze them, to attempt to straighten them out. Along with their peculiarities, all their qualities also disappear. Any kind of creation exhausts the creator so much that they need more than one day in seven to rest. Their indulgence in little peculiarities help them to restore themselves.

~

There was a young lady who used to be seen daily at lunch at a table near one of the pillars in the Rose Room, always with a book propped up in front of her and a cigarette in a long, amber cigarette holder. She was tall, very blonde, round-faced, with a peaches-and-cream complexion, and wore the most florid hats any woman ever wore. When she moved her hands, the tinkling of the rows of bracelets on her wrists never failed to attract attention. She looked as if she had just stepped out of the *Floradora* chorus. The waiters addressed her as "Countess."

Her blue eyes roamed above her book while she ate, read, and smoked at the same time. If she caught anybody's glance directed at her, she responded with a warm smile. As soon as her table was cleared of dishes, she took an elaborate notebook and gold pen from her handbag and preceded to write furiously, with the graceful attitudes of a writer in deep thought, as shown on the stage or in the movies, and only interrupted her labors from time to time to look up, to see if she was being seen, again acknowledging a glance with a broad smile. How she ever expected to attract attention in a roomful of writers by reading a book or writing, only she alone could tell. She wasn't less beautiful than many beautiful women in the dining room, but nobody ever spoke to her despite all her come-hither smiles and the fluttering of her long lashes.

After a while, having taken her own acknowledgment of having been seen as a form of acquaintanceship, when she passed by a table she nodded to those to whom she had smiled previously. It was an odd way to court friendship, but she was very persistent and carried on the same process every day, month after month. The only people who talked to her were the waiters, the bellboys, and the elevator men. When there were strangers in the dining room, she had herself paged: "Countess Solini . . . Countess Solini!"

One day, a middle-aged actor, annoyed by her table manners, went to her table while she was at the phone and looked at what she had written. And, just as he had expected, no doubt, he saw words, one after the other, without sense or connection: words, words, words. She was furious when she returned and saw him with her notebook in his hands, then laughed and left, never to be seen again in the Rose Room.

Months later, I saw her at the Brown Derby in Hollywood, where she was repeating the same procedure as at the Algonquin. When I went to Malibu for a swim, she was there, stretched out in the sand, face down, in all her Titian splendor, her Rubenesque figure encased in a bathing suit, a cigarette holder between her teeth, dark glasses, a book to the right, a pad and gold pencil on her left. I saw her again in Paris, on the terrace of the Deux Maggots, with a book propped in front of her and a pad and a pen beside her. She had become a fixture there. I have often wondered on what and how she lived. My curiosity almost drove me to speak to her in Paris, but I feared she had set her cap for a writer, any writer, anywhere, of any race, color, or nationality.

She was a rather good-looking, ripe blonde and would have suc-ceeded in acquiring the kind of man she desired had she used subtler tactics. Why she insisted on calling attention through a book and a pad is more than I can understand. She is probably still at it, somewhere, in London, Copenhagen, Cairo, or Berlin; or she may have stopped writing and discarded the bait after catching the fish.

~

The Round Table of the Algonquin Rose Room has been famous now for many, many years. People have spoken and written about it as a most unique institution. Young writers all over the country think of it as a sort of goal, and would consider themselves arrived and successful only after they, too, were privileged to sit at the Round Table to discuss literature with the celebrities.

The Round Table came into being some thirty-odd years ago. Heywood Broun, Alexander Woollcott, Laurence Stallings, Deems Taylor, and Franklin P. Adams, all working on the *New York World* at the time, gathered at a table, a round one as it happened, every noon. Since each one of them had some power to direct attention to the work of other people, the tale spread that decisions as to whose works should be praised were made right there, in a sort of conspiracy. The Round Table had no sooner become famous, than it became a byword. Some people called it the log-rolling table. When Deems Taylor, the music critic of the *New York World*, praised a piece of music or the performance of a musician in his column, the envious promptly spread the news that so and so "has friends at the Round Table." If the praised musician was a woman, you can imagine what other women singers gossiped about. If Taylor commented unfavorably, the disgruntled one said she had enemies at the Round Table. What was said about Deems Taylor also applied to Laurence Stallings, who was the chief book reviewer of the *New York World*, and to Woollcott, the drama critic, and to Broun and F.P.A., who roamed over all the intellectual fields.

There was, no doubt, some log-rolling. The consortium held people of strong opinions, who, when they liked someone's work or disliked it, went all-out in their praise or condemnation. So, after a while, the people of the Round Table were looked upon as a sort of a monstrous, monolithic monopoly of the arts, and jealous columnists on other papers, by damning it enhanced its reputation. The gossip column came into existence about thirty years ago; the columnists took years to develop the technique of their métier before they stopped talking only about each other.

Eventually a few other literary figures joined the Round Table as steady guests: Marc Connelly, Harold Ross, editor of the *New Yorker*, George and Beatrice Kaufman, Bob Benchley, Robert Sherwood, Ernest Boyd, Dorothy Parker, Margalo Gillmore, and Edna Ferber. The truth is that literary or musical subjects were seldom discussed at that table. These people came for relaxation, rest from labors performed, and the talk was more frequently about poker and tennis than about books and the arts.

Heywood Broun attracted more attention than anybody else, and not only because of his huge, disarming, and quaint personality. A lumbering hulk of a man, he walked with the grace of an elephant. Dishes often clattered to the floor as he brushed by the tables of the dining room. He just couldn't make his way from the door to the Round Table at the other side without coming into contact with chairs and tables. He had a thin, perpetually hoarse voice, which became shrill when he was aroused or amused. When he wasn't talking about sports, he was trying to explain politics. An extreme liberal, considered a revolutionary, he was perpetually arguing with the more conservative elements at the table. A profoundly religious man, he used sharp language, but never profanity, not under any provocation, and would leave the table, even the room, when it was used in his presence. He tolerated and often used Rabelaisian language, but not profanity. If Rabelais was often called "the profane Homer," Broun could have answered to the nickname of "the religious Rabelais."

Broun's column in the *New York World* attracted considerable attention, and people often came to the hotel just to have a look at him. When he felt lonesome, he sat down near the first stranger in the lobby, engaging him in conversation, and ordering drinks. He smoked incessantly, but seldom carried cigarettes with him. Enjoying complete freedom of expression in the paper, he often expressed views which were in strong contradiction with the policy of the *New York World*.

In 1921, when Queen Marie of Romania visited the United States, she contracted for a daily column in which to describe her impressions of America, to be published by the *New York World* and its syndicate. A dollar-grabbing and commercially unscrupulous lady, she also signed a contract with a second syndicate and saw her trunks seized until she, or the embassy, settled the affair. Her columns were childish in the extreme, and had she not been a queen, and a queen with a reputation not based on her literary talents, no paper would have published a line of what she wrote; stupid, ungrammatical, and dull stuff.

Since her column was placed next to Broun's, he was annoyed by his neighbor on the same page, as he would have been had she actually lived in the same house with him. At that time, that page of the *New York World* was filled by a company of writers never duplicated before or since, in any newspaper. F. P. A., Stallings, Taylor, and Woollcott were all writing daily columns, and H. G. Wells was a guest columnist. Queen

Figure 21. Queen Marie of Romania, c. 1920s. *Source*: Library of Congress, Prints and Photographs Division.

Marie, in all her glorious ineptitude, was added to them. They all felt bitter about it. And so, one day, Broun wrote a piece about his royal neighbor and said what he had wanted to say for a long time, pointing out how illiterate she was, how untrue her stuff was, how childish, and that it would never have been published if Marie weren't a queen. It was bad writing, queen or no queen, and he didn't like her and her stuff.

I can well imagine that, in manuscript, Heywood's column was even more uncomplimentary than in the printed version. I can hear the bickering between the editor and Broun, with Broun making a concession here and there, but pointing to the contract with the *New York World* which gave him the right to express his personal views unhampered, uncensored. That morning's column was like a cleansing wind and increased the reputation of the *New York World* a hundredfold. Broun's column proved to the readers that every writer on the paper had complete freedom to express their views, but patriotic Romanians in New York City were outraged. At noon, a large group, in their colorful national costumes, carrying placards denouncing Broun, milled in front of the Algonquin Hotel, and attracted a considerable crowd.

Totally disregarding the fact that he was the butt of the Romanians, Broun lumbered through them, smiling, then stood at the door and watched them parade up and down. For years he had been picketing on every possible occasion, for every possible cause, to help strikers, to denounce the actions of the British in India, to protest against infractions of civil liberties, and now he was himself being picketed; and he enjoyed it. Entering the lobby he stopped everyone, friends, acquaintances, strangers—everyone—and pulled them out to point out that he was being picketed. It was great fun. He threw his hat down—a hat always at least two sizes too small for his head—and stamped on it. "By all the rickety, brickety papersnappers, I am being picketed!"

Heywood was generous with his money when there was a cause to support, but he was not the man who eagerly grabbed a check from the waiter. As a matter of fact, he often looked the other way when the tab was presented. But that day he asked everybody to have a drink on him. The Queen had made herself obnoxious to many people, and they were glad she had been shown up. Eventually Gene Fowler, too, did a good job on her, after being her choice on a transcontinental trip with twenty more reporters on the train.

Broun had been carrying on an active campaign against the proposed legal murder of Sacco and Vanzetti. There came a time when the editors and managers of the *New York World* thought he had gone too far and refused to print one of his columns. Broun stood his ground, insisted on his rights, and, since the management persisted in its attitude, he broke his contract with the paper. To cut the ground from under him, a banner headline appeared on the front page the following morning with the announcement: "Heywood Broun Dismissed From the *New York World*."

That banner made Heywood the hero of all the liberals in the city and in the country. At lunchtime, people stood in line in the lobby of the hotel to shake his hand. A rival paper offered Broun the privilege of stating his case. He accepted and explained in his inimitable way what had happened. He pointed out that the loss of salary would not exactly beggar him. Year after year he had won a certain amount of money in poker, and that alone was enough to keep him in moderate circumstances: an occasional piece in a magazine would help to keep him in luxuries. "But," said he, "even if I never played poker again, and no magazine would take my articles, I'd still do as I am doing rather than be told what I may and may not write."

What Heywood Broun possessed to a higher degree than ninety-nine percent of all newspapermen was character. Though most of those at the Round Table disagreed with his political opinions, they approved of his intransigent position, admired his integrity, and he became a hero even in their eyes. Shortly after Broun's dismissal, the *New York World*, compelled by the loss of circulation, asked him to come back to the fold. Broun consented, but on one condition: that the article which they had refused to publish be the first one printed. And it was. The *New York World* ate crow. I remember a party with a circle of friends dancing around him, and he, like an elephant, raising first one foot and then the other, clapping his hands, laughing, and shrilling: "Funds are needed to save Sacco and Vanzetti." They were not saved. The day of their execution was a sad day for Broun, for many other liberals, for America.

Figure 22. Caricature of Alexander Woollcott by Miguel Corubias, 1924. *Source*: Library of Congress, Prints and Photographs Division.

Woollcott, too, was a center of attraction. There was zest, power, and verbal felicity in almost everything he wrote. In life he was a sophisticated boy who had not grown up; a turbulent sophisticate who loved to shock people even with sentimentality. He was one of the first men of literary distinction to become a radio speaker. The "Town Crier" was among the first of the radio commentators and storytellers. Across the table, as in his drama reviews, Woollcott had rather a sharp manner of expressing himself. A born actor, he loved to hear himself talk and be the center of attention. His opinions on many things were often as outrageous as they were well phrased, in a Chestertonian style. With a superb command of adjectives, which he wielded like so many rapiers, he was a dangerous verbal duelist. On the radio he used a most mellifluous voice and told or retold the most sentimental stories about cats and dogs and their devotion.

He and Michael Arlen, of *Green Hat* fame, then at the pinnacle of that fame, were great friends, and they were often side by side at the Round Table. However, something or other in Arlen annoyed Heywood Broun, probably because Arlen affected his Englishness, or because he mentioned too often all the titled ladies he knew. There was also talk of a poker party at the Thanatopsis Club, housed in the Algonquin building, in which Arlen had won a considerable amount of money from Broun. Whatever good can be said of Broun, he was a bad loser. He played to win and not for sport. He crowed when he won, but was sarcastic and angry when he lost.

A most scathing analysis of one of Arlen's books in Broun's column caused a coolness between Woollcott and Broun. While that lasted, Woollcott would come to the entrance of the dining room and turn away if he saw Broun at the table . . . turn away, accompanied by Broun's guffaws.

There were other Round Tables, both in the Rose Room and in the Oak Room. There was, and still is, a table at which Dr. Frank Kingdon, Louis Nizer, Harry Hershfield, Jesse Lasky, when he is in town, *Film Daily* editor Jack Alicoate, and Martin Quigley, editor of *Motion Picture Daily*, hold forth. Jimmy Walker, Fiorella LaGuardia, the present mayor of New York, O'Dwyer, and many other celebrities were guests at that table. Columnists Leonard Lyons and Earl Wilson, of the *New York*

Post, joined in the discussions. The subjects most often discussed there are local and national politics, and philosophical and scientific subjects, when prominent philosophers and scientists are guests of one or another of the habitués. On Saturdays, splendiferous Marcella, Kingdon's wife, and beautiful Mildred, Nizer's wife, join the company.

Elliott Roosevelt, his wife and their friends, and occasionally Mrs. Eleanor Roosevelt, occupy an adjoining table. Although they are not there every day, the table is held for them for a reasonable time by Raul, the Oak Room captain, who says that Mrs. Roosevelt is the most beautiful woman, spiritually. Jack Alicoate, the Colonel, as he is called, presides, but Louis Nizer is the arbiter. Dr. Kingdon, who in his own way is as uncompromising as was Heywood Broun, holds sway in every discussion. A former minister and former college president, Kingdon is accustomed to being listened to. His booming voice is heard clear across the room. He tolerates all opinions as long as he believes them to be sincere; but woe to anybody in whom he detects a tinge of insincerity. On such occasions his scorn becomes Homeric and only Louis Nizer, the suavest of men, can reestablish order.

The Round Table in the Oak Room seats about eight people comfortably, but on occasion twice as many crowd around it. Before and after every important national or international event the atmosphere is heavy. There are as many opinions at that table as there are people, and no holds are barred. Louis Nizer either starts a discussion or sums it up. His summings up are masterly. He gathers all the ends, the loose ones especially, and weaves them into a conclusive strand. When he breaks into a discussion, he uses the Socratic manner and method of confusing the witness with his own answers.

Ben Bodne, the new owner, joins the table when he is invited, and listens. When interested in a discussion, he won't leave that table no matter how urgent his appearance elsewhere may be: "Tell him I'll call him back later."

"But the call is from Texas!"

"I don't care if it's from India. I'll call back later."

I have known men to miss trains and planes because they couldn't tear themselves away from the Round Table in the Oak Room.

Another steady guest at the Kingdon, Alicoate, Nizer table is Elmer Leterman, the famous insurance man. The authors at the table have, in him, their best customer. Whenever he brings a guest, he buys for them every book the authors have written and has them autographed for his guest. Everyone at the table gets pocketbooks, pen knives, pencils, and fountain pens, free, from Leterman, who seldom opens his mouth in a discussion. When he does, everybody looks up: "Hear, hear. Elmer has spoken!"

Alice Hughes, the columnist, has her own table. Alice loves to recite poetry and can also listen to it by the hour, even in languages she only half understands; I know, because I have walked the streets many a night with her, reciting argot and Greek poetry to her.

~

When I was a student in Milan, I stayed at the pension Mirandelo: five floors of house, situated in the center of a long court. The kitchen and the dining room were on the ground floor. The floor above was inhabited by the sculptors. Above them lived the musicians. Singers were on the third floor, writers on the fourth. The top floor was occupied by the Mirandelo family, and the garret by the cooks and servants. At the farthest end of the court, there was a long shed in which the sculptors plied their art.

Signor Mirandelo never took his meals with us. He departed at noon, with cane and gloves, and no one knew where he went or what he did. We didn't get much food for the little money we paid. Still, out of this little money, Mrs. Mirandelo had saved enough to buy a castle on the Mediterranean; a magnificent old castle to which Mussolini later on retired from his labors, accompanied by some willing young lady. There wasn't much furniture in our rooms. The mattresses were hard, the linen was changed once a month, and the blankets were like sieves. As for cleanliness, the less said about it the better. If one acquired a girlfriend from among the young actresses or singers, she took care of the room, the sewing of buttons, and the laundry. But we were all young, and what was left empty by the scanty food was filled by hope and dreams of the future. Whenever we protested against the scantiness of the victuals, Mrs. Mirandelo reproached us our crass materialism and spoke of the past generation of students who had lived at the pension on much less food than we were getting, yet had made something of themselves: "You think of food, food, all the time. You should eat to live; not live to eat!"

Signora Mirandelo weighed in the neighborhood of 250 pounds, though she was forever dieting, on a pound of chocolates between lunch and dinner. She was by far the most voluminous, voluble woman I have known. To the sculptors she would say: "All you think about is food.

Auguste Rodin lived here. He never protested about the food." Then, to the singers: "Do you know that the very room you occupy Caruso once occupied? Mascagni lived here, and there you are, protesting that you don't get enough, when Mascagni composed his *Cavelleria Rusticana* in the room you are now occupying. What have you done in that famous room? Madonna mia! Food! Food!" After every one of these protests, there was a little more bread on the table and a little more spaghetti in the dish, for a week or ten days, then the portions came down to the usual subnormal normal. She was very economical with cheese, but what there was of it was strong.

Mrs. Mirandelo presided over the table and entertained us with stories of the glorious people who had once been her pensionnaires to make us forget the absence of meat and the thinness of the minestrone. We supplemented the meals by raiding the kitchen at night, stealing a ham or a side of bacon which we shared and ate raw. Caruso, we were told, had once stolen and cooked Mrs. Mirandelo's parrot, and it was a known fact that Rodin had made similar use of one of her cats. The story was that the window of Caruso's room was over the window with the parrot's perch. On a Sunday, when Mrs. Mirandelo was away, Caruso lifted the parrot off the perch, with a fisherman's hook. Rodin got the cat by a simpler method and had a better meal.

Other pensions in the neighborhood, charging the same one hundred liras ($20) a month for everything except laundry, with cleaner rooms and more food, did not have the reputation of the Mirandelo pension. The pensionnaires of the Mirandelo looked down on the guests of the other places, who could not boast of a Rodin, a Mascagni, and a Caruso as former pensionnaires.

There was a room on the top floor which Mrs. Mirandelo showed to new guests, when a room was vacated by a student gone to fame or home to die of inanition. Short and heavy, with a tremendous, heaving bosom, she would climb up the rickety staircase to show that room which had, at one time, housed Eleanora Duse, the great Italian dramatic actress. Occasionally she would show the trunkful of clothes which had once belonged to La Duse. She didn't tell how she had come into possession of the trunk: that she had retained it when La Duse hadn't had enough money to pay for her month's pension. There were other trunks in the attic and in the cellar, trunks and bags of less famous people than La Duse, but they were shown only to students requesting an extension of credit. "I am not hard-hearted, but I have no space left for another trunk. See for yourself. Madonna mia! Where will I put it? No! No credit." What kept most students there was the atmosphere and the legends, true or untrue, of the people who had once lived in those rooms and starved at that long oak table.

There were no idlers at the Mirandelo. No one played at art. Each one had a goal; each one hoped to follow in the footsteps of some of the successful artists who had once lived there. One didn't have to live in Rodin's room to become a great sculptor, or in Caruso's room to become a great singer: just the same, I wouldn't have given up Mascagni's room for any other room in the world. Against one of the walls was an old, rickety piano, which I had to learn how to tune myself, because it ran out of tune under my fingers. But in despondent moments, I looked at that piano, remembered that Mascagni had written his immortal *Cavelleria Rusticana* at it, and my hopes and ambitions were renewed. He, too, had had to tune that piano.

Years later, the famous Italian playwright Luigi Pirandello told me he had seen my name on the books of the pension in Milan, and that Mrs. Mirandelo, older and fatter, had shown him the piano and told him that for a time a young man who became a writer in America had lived there. I was a deserter in her eyes: to have occupied Mascagni's room for two years without having become a musician was a crime. This kind of superstition exists among all artists. My teacher, Charles Maria Widor, pointing to the organ at St. Sulpice in Paris at which he had officiated for seventy-five years, said: "When you touch this, you touch the keyboard on which the greatest organists have played, myself included. When I'll be no more, people will say: 'this is the organ on which Widor played.' And they'll draw inspiration from it. I went to Germany to look at the organ Bach played on, and drew from it the inspiration for my Toccata and Fugue."

≈

The Algonquin is not the pension Mirandelo. One couldn't live there on twenty dollars a month, but there are as many legends about its rooms as about the place in Milan. Not that there is a floor for sculptors and another for musicians and one for singers or actors. Frank Case, on occasion, received a half-interest in a play from a playwright who couldn't pay his bills. Raul, the headwaiter, got the rights to another play in payment for a dinner, but I doubt whether the cellar holds any trunks of the famous of yesteryear.

That Frank Case, who had been its boniface, should have fostered some of the legends can be readily understood. That the new owner, Ben B. Bodne, who had been in the oil business, which is as far from any of the arts as any business can be, should have acquired a certain attitude towards his own rooms in the last few years is little short of amazing. A great admirer of Rex Beach, who is seldom in New York, Mr. Bodne showed me the suite Beach occupies when he comes to the city, and added: "The other day I put a couple in here and told them that Rex Beach usually occupies it when he is in the city.

"'Rex Beach? Who is that?' the man asked. If there had been another suite vacant, I would have moved them out of there. Fancy that! They hadn't even heard of Rex Beach! That suite was just wasted on them. Many people would be happy to say, truthfully, that they had had Mr. Beach's suite in New York."

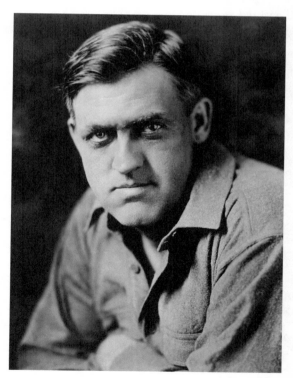

Figure 23. Rex Beach. *Source*: Bain News Service, Library of Congress, Prints and Photographs Division.

Some forty years ago, Eugene Walter came from the West, where he had been working at many things, including journalism, with the idea for a play in his head. He moved to the Algonquin, and during a conversation over something or other in a glass, he told Frank of his ambition and outlined the plot of the play. Frank thought it was great. Case thought all plays were great, even the bad ones, particularly in the presence of the playwright. The idea of a man manipulating the movements of people on a stage and giving them words to say was fascinating: "It takes guts to even begin a play, let alone finish it."

Though Walter isolated himself in his room for weeks, the work did not progress. He just couldn't pass the hurdle of the second act in the play. When his money gave out, he got a job with a theatrical company, as its advance agent, and traveled for months all over the country. The play he advertised and press-agented was worthless, but it was Walter's job to tout it, to praise it, to talk it up to newspaper critics and managers. He

Figure 24. Eugene Walter, c. 1920s. *Source*: Bain News Service, Library of Congress, Prints and Photographs Division.

lived on very little, not using up even his expense account, and when he had saved enough money to go back to New York, he dropped the job and returned to his room, which Case assured him was a lucky room, and went back to work on the play. This time the play progressed: in the language of playwrights, "it wrote itself." In less than two months, it was finished and read to friends, who assured him it was great. Meanwhile, his money had again given out; but Case, who believed in him and the play, extended credit: "Don't worry. You'll pay it all back."

When the play began to make the rounds of the producers, what had seemed to be the least important of all things turned out to be the most difficult one. The first producer turned it down cold: "It's a good play, but not the kind I like." Frank's own judgment was not shaken, and credit was further extended while the play was sent to a second producer. For a while it looked as though it would go into production, but at the last minute the producer returned the play: "The backer couldn't see it."

There was another long wait while the play went to a third producer. And when the third producer refused it, Walter, instead of coming down to the dining room three times a day, began to skip one meal. When a fourth producer refused it, he skipped two meals and eventually lived on coffee and bread which he got at a cafeteria, after pawning his watch and typewriter. It is not known to how many producers the play went, and how many refused it, but when at last a letter of acceptance arrived, Walter hadn't been in his room for days. The story goes that he was discovered on a park bench and was so weak, he was made weaker by the good news and had to be carried bodily to his room. When he recovered, his friend was standing over him, saying: "I told you the room is a lucky one. Do you believe it now?" The play, *Paid in Full*, did make Eugene Walter affluent, even after he paid his debts. He moved out to the Connecticut hills, but came back from time to time to finish a play, always to the same lucky room.

After many years in Hollywood, Elmer Harris, the author of *Johnny Belinda*, now lives in the wilds of Canada, where he can shoot at wild geese in their flight from off the porch of his house. But he still comes to New York to put the finishing touches on his plays. Nobody can call Elmer Harris a superstitious man; I'd say he is the least superstitious person I have ever met. He laughs at himself about the "Algonquin business": "All this talk about atmosphere is all nonsense. I don't see anyone's spirit floating about. But I work better in a certain room than in any other one. Can you tell me why this is so?"

The late Bayard Veiller, author of *The Thirteenth Chair*, idled away a week once, waiting for a certain room to be vacated, protesting: "I wired from California that I was coming. Frank should have known the room I wanted. I can't work in the room he gave me."

Dorothy Spears, author, singer, and now professor of literature at Boston University, said:

"I don't know what it is about this place. Do you? But here I am."

$\sim$

At the end of the second World War, a handsome young man with a Christ-like face and beard used to come into the lobby and sit on a sofa, thin hands folded. No one knew him. He never ate in the dining room and didn't live at the hotel. One day, a lady from California staying at the hotel asked Case, "Do you know who that young man is?"

"No," said Frank. "But I've seen him here on and off. I've thought about him. He looks so different from most of the people who come here. Who is he? Do you know?"

"Well, he is the Messiah," the woman said.

Frank was a very religious man and didn't like talk about the Messiah being bandied about, but a guest of the hotel was a guest of the hotel, and so Frank inquired very politely: "What makes you say he is the Messiah? Are you judging him by his looks?"

"He told me so. He has a message for the world. He wants to save it."

"I'm glad to hear somebody wants to save the world," Case said, moving away. There was always somebody to call Case to the telephone when he was being cornered or bored by one of the guests. Managers and astute bellboys were there to protect Frank Case from bores.

The following day, women grouped about that young Messiah, who talked to them, orating far above a whisper. When this performance had been repeated several days in succession, the lobby began to look like a mission house. The young man raised his voice, carried away by his own eloquence, and pounded a fist in his palm as he enumerated the sins of the world, a whole dictionary of sins. The day after, when a group of strange women had crowded the lobby again, Frank Case intercepted the Messiah at the door and said to him: "Young man, this is the lobby of a hotel, and not a church."

Some of the women followed the young man, who left without argument. When they were all gone, a little old lady, who had been watching from a distance without joining the crowd, said to Case: "I don't believe that young man is the Messiah. He is either a deluded man or an impostor."

"That's what I was thinking," Frank said, glad to hear his judgment confirmed.

"But what I am thinking," the little old lady added, "is, that if he were the real Messiah, would you have recognized him as such? Wouldn't you have turned him out, also? Do you realize what has happened to us? We wouldn't recognize Him if He came. Shouldn't we rather make a thousand errors than turn Him away from the door?"

The words of that little old lady left an indelible impression on Frank Case. He told me the story again and again. I gathered the impression there never had been a little old lady; that she was Frank Case's invention, through whom he retold one of the greatest of all parables. Like the French painter Steinlen, who once exhibited a picture of Christ being stopped at the entrance of Notre Dame because of his poverty-stricken appearance.

Frank told me a number of stories about people he had met for the first time and thought they were deluded, impostors, or whose faith in themselves was not justified. People who had eventually turned out to be what he had thought they were not. Again and again he had promised himself not to rely on first judgment: "I hired a chef once who recommended himself so highly, I didn't believe one-tenth of what he said. But I needed someone and thought I'd give him the job until I found someone else. He turned out to be everything he said he was, and much more, and worked for me many years."

Some people in the arts have taken the advice not to hide their light under a bushel much too literally, but every so often one reads about some whose self-assertion, and often arrogance, is justified by the work they produce. Leopold Godowsky said that when he was one of the judges in a competition instituted by a radio company in conjunction with a publishing house, he found among the musical manuscripts sent to the committee a rather badly mauled folder in which there was a letter from the composer. In it, he stated that not only was his composition far and above any produced in this generation, it easily measured up to the compositions of the great masters of all times: "If my composition doesn't win the prize, it won't be a reflection on my work, but on the judges, and history will know how to judge them."

"And so," Godowsky said, "what do you do when you get a letter like that? Instead of reading the manuscript, you show the letter to your colleagues and remark on the impudence of the young fellows of this generation. It's true that Beethoven, on occasion, wrote more or less similar letters in his day; but then, he was Beethoven. The letter said, in effect: 'I am a genius.' When a man says that, you are ninety-nine percent sure he is anything but. My first impulse was to drop the manuscript into a wastepaper basket and forget about it. Reflecting on this and that, the thought occurred to me that I had been pretty sure of myself when I was young; that although I didn't go about telling the world I was a genius, I had a pretty high estimation of my ability and talent. When an artist doesn't feel that what he is doing is great, there is no reason for him to do it. If anybody else can do it as well or better, why should an artist try to do that particular thing?

"So, not doubting that my original opinion of the author would be confirmed, I put the manuscript on the piano and began to play it. And what do you think? It was as good as he said it was: a most extraordinary piece of work, original; powerful, well-conceived, well carried out. There wasn't another composition in the lot half as good as that one. I still resented the letter. Why should a young man who had such talent feel it necessary to shout it to the world? I wrote a letter to the composer, asking him to come and see me, and found him to be a very modest young man when we were face to face!"

I'm telling this story, not to show how deceptive appearances are, but to give some idea of the kind of people one comes up against when one mingles with creative artists. That is why they are so often considered freaks. That is why the average man, unaccustomed to such self-assertion, shies away from them. Yet, somehow, in the last decade or two, the blatant advertisements in the papers and magazines, the large posters on walls and along railroad tracks, barring the view of the landscape, praising all kinds of merchandise, every one claiming "this is the best"; the blatant publicity and trumpeting around every little effort shows that self-assertion is one of the sins of modern competitive life. Even as great a man as van Loon didn't hesitate to shove aside all other historians and proclaim himself the best, and when no one sang his praises in his presence, he would wind up by saying: "You see? If I didn't do it myself, who would?"

～

After long years of serving writers, one of the waiters took it into his head that he, too, could be a playwright. He didn't believe that the people he served were more intelligent than he was, or that they knew more about life than he did: "If B. can write a play, so can I."

After seeing many plays, he concluded that none of them were better, or even as good as he could write: and he had ideas. To begin with, his own life would make a great play. And so, having accumulated a little money, he left his job, and, to bolster himself up as belonging to the fraternity, began to appear at the Algonquin for lunch, to sit at the same table with men whose meals he had once served, and to talk shop with them. He had learned enough of the theatrical jargon to sound like a professional.

Eventually he wrote a play, and either because it was not good enough, or for other reasons, it was not accepted by the first, the second, or the third producer. When his money gave out, he went back to work as a waiter, but at another restaurant, where nobody knew him. He still lunched at the Algonquin on his day off, telling his new writer-friends that someone was dickering for his play, that he had rejected a movie contract, that there were casting difficulties, and so on.

The first time one of the usual habitués of the Algonquin dropped in, by chance, at the restaurant where the waiter-playwright was serving was also the last time any of us ever saw him in New York. I met him years later, in a restaurant in Texas.

Raul, the headwaiter of the Oak Room, writes lyrics and songs. He is also forever investing small sums of money in plays and considers himself slighted when one of his guests hasn't shown him the manuscript of a play before it is produced for his opinion, or to give him a chance to invest a little money. So far he has invested only in flops. Raul, an Argentinian Italian, speaks several languages fluently. He is the soul of the Oak Room, where he is a master at seating people in the worst section of the room, while giving them the feeling that they are favored guests. He is also a musician and plays several instruments. "I am the Caruso of the banjo," he says.

Georges, the former headwaiter of the Rose Room, wrote a book. There was considerable publicity about it, but it never appeared in print. While there may have been other contributing factors as to why Georges left the Algonquin, I have a suspicion that the many inquiries about the date of publication had their effect on him.

There was another waiter, an educated Greek, who wrote political articles for the local Greek papers and an occasional letter to the *New York Times*. He usually carried the clippings in his pockets, showed them around and explained: "I am not a waiter who writes. I am a writer who waits. Peter Altenberg was also a waiter, and the present British poet-laureate cleaned cuspidors in a Greenwich Village saloon."

~

Since most of their clients live or dine at the Algonquin, literary and theatrical agents have made the hotel their meeting ground. When you see one of them with a client, it is because a story has been sold or a play has been contracted for or an actor has gotten a part. Ten percenters don't waste time. They often appear with a new client as a hands-off warning to other agents. When an agent, writer, and editor lunch together, it's in the bag; the sale has been made. Writers are the least jealous or envious of mortals. Any professional writer is glad to see another one get his due or a chance at what is coming to them.

It is unethical for an agent to lure a client away from another agent, so they avoid being unethical to the letter, but not the spirit. Since there are at present more women than men literary and theatrical agents, the man-made ethics are often disregarded by the ladies. However, a writer, as well as a playwright or an actor, drops their agent when they haven't done them any good for a long time. It is ethical for both writer and agent to act as if they had mutually agreed to disagree, and one would be hard put to find a writer, actor, or playwright who has gone back to his original agent after trying another one. Agents and their clients hang on to each other as long as they are mutually profitable.

There are few bona-fide agents who take on a new writer, but there are many who charge a fee for reading the manuscripts of new writers. The Algonquin is the home, at lunchtime, of literary agents. Agents were not as necessary, formerly, but now they are so well entrenched it is fairly impossible to deal directly with an editor, producer, or director of a play: it has to be done through an agent. If you do get a play to a producer by yourself and he likes it, the first question he asks is: "Who is your agent?"

Some of the Hollywood producers are copartners of certain agencies . . . not a very ethical arrangement, but Hollywood has its own code of ethics.

No matter how you operate, an agent will get ten percent of your earnings. Some agents claim to have influence with this or that editor or publisher. The truth is that they can only sell what is marketable. An editor who would buy a story or a novel only because he likes the agent or the author would soon find himself out on his ear. Editors make mistakes, but they only accept material they believe is fit for publication.

The story is told of an agent who stood in the lobby of a theatre during an opening night performance, watching a number of his clients coming out during the intermission, and remarked to a friend: "There go the so-and-so's who take away my ninety percent. Look at them, all dressed up: the men in cutaways, the women in new gowns and platinum bracelets on their wrists. All out of my ninety percent!"

The late Otto Liveright was an exception among agents. He had a "stable" of most distinguished writers: Hendrik van Loon, H. G. Wells, Don Byrne, Theodore Dreiser, Helen Miller, Nunnally Johnson, Charles Brackett, and Franchot Tone, who at one time was very eager to establish himself as a writer. It was Otto who suggested to Tone that he would do better as an actor than as a writer.

Otto was a very sensitive little man and easily offended. A loud word upset him; a slighting remark would send him to bed for a week. Frank Case used to say: "I am afraid to say good morning to him, lest my tone of voice offend him."

Then, one day, I saw him lunching with Jim Tully, the ex-prize-fighter whose stories were not at all the kind Otto liked to handle. What distinguished Otto from other agents was the fact that he never offered a story for sale that he himself didn't like. His percentage of sales was the highest of any agent. The mere fact that he agreed to handle a story practically guaranteed its sale. He had a keen critical faculty and didn't hesitate to argue with his most famous writers, and point out defects in stories and novels which had to be remedied before he took the work to a publisher or an editor. He did that at the risk of losing his most valuable clients. He was more insistent with the well-known than with the lesser known, just to convince himself of his integrity. Otto often suspected himself more than he suspected others and had a hard time living with himself. When Otto accepted three stories in a row from a writer without offering any suggestions, he began to think that he was going downhill. The second table to the right in the Rose Room was his permanent table for years. At that table—and not in his office—he argued with his writers.

Those of us who knew Otto well wondered at seeing him with the pugnacious redhead: wondered, because we didn't know whether it was Jim Tully who had been able to improve his style so as to conform to Otto's standards, or Otto who had lowered his standards to please Jim.

This went on for quite a while. They were steady companions at lunch, talking earnestly while they ate. There was no sharper contrast imaginable between two individuals than between those two men. Otto was thin, a wisp of a man, very dark, with the manners of a petulant prince. Jim was short and squat, redheaded, unmannerly, a loud talker, and generally looked as though he had just come out of a third-rate arena. Otto dressed immaculately. Jim took pride in his dishevelment.

Then, one day, Otto sat by himself at his table and made it quite clear by his behavior that he didn't want anybody to join him. Jim lunched at another table, at the other end of the room. When I asked Otto what had happened, he said: "He was as sweet as an angel until I sold one of his stories. I worked with him on that story for weeks. It had a good idea. And for a prizefighter, he behaved well and was polite. He no sooner got his first check than he became the most arrogant pup I have ever known, and out of a clear sky began to give me his 'unvarnished' opinion of all the writers I handle, and of the advice I had given him. I have never seen such a change in a man."

Sometime later, Jim Tully, whom I had known many years before his name meant anything to the reading public, explained what had happened in terms of the prize ring: "It is as I am. I can be friends with a guy until I beat him. But after that, I can't look him in the eye and I hate him. I never allowed my manager to rematch me with a guy I had beaten, partly because I couldn't stand the idea that maybe he would beat me next time. When I put a guy down, I want him to stay down."

"But what has that got to do with Otto?" I asked.

"Well, he was my manager, wasn't he? And I had to take it from him. Do the story this way, do the story that way. I don't have to take it from him anymore, and I can't look him in the eye, thinking of all the yessing I had to do until he sold that story for me. Now I'll look for another agent, who didn't help me, to whom I am champ. See? I just can't look a guy in the eye after I've beaten him "

"But you admit he has helped *you*."

"Yeah, but he's also seen me being knocked down, when an editor wouldn't accept my story."

Poor Jim! He didn't sell many stories afterwards, though he changed agents after every sale they made for him.

Jim lived at the Algonquin when he was in New York and wanted it known. He sent dozens of postcards to people who had beaten him and to the ones he had beaten and invited them to come and see him.

He occupied one room; I had a suite. He met his guests in the lobby and then took them up to my quarters without asking me. Being visited once by a pug, on whom he wanted to make an impression, he told him I was his secretary, and ordered me about: "Get me that ashtray." When the phone rang, he said: "See who it is. I'll call back later. I'm too busy."

I left my rooms. When I returned, the pug was fast asleep in my bed; Jim was gone. He was in H. L. Mencken's suite. He liked Mencken. Somebody had called him the Mencken of the West.

~

In the days when the Beethoven Association was housed in the annex of the Algonquin, many musicians lunched daily in one or the other of the dining rooms. On one of his last visits to the United States, I invited the late Ignace Paderewski to have breakfast with me. He had been host to me on his ranch in California, and I wanted to return the compliment in my humble manner. Paderewski was willing. He wanted to talk to me about Poland. "Let's go where I won't be recognized, where people won't stare at me; where we can sit quietly and talk without anybody coming over for an autograph, or to interview me. I've had too much of that of late."

I assured him we could eat in peace at the Algonquin. Nobody would try to interview him or ask for his autograph: nobody was ever bothered for such things at the Algonquin. "That's fine," Paderewski said. "Let's have breakfast there. Eight o'clock, if it's not too early for you."

Besides being a great pianist, Paderewski was also a statesman. He had been president of the Polish Republic and had a grasp of international politics few men possessed. We no sooner sat down when he launched into the story of his presidency and recalled the conversations he had had with President Wilson in Paris, during the Versailles conference. It was out of these conversations with Wilson that the Polish Republic emerged at the end of World War I. Paderewski was an irresistible person, of great charm, and an inimitable raconteur. It was common knowledge that President Wilson wouldn't have stood so fast on the question of Polish independence had it not been for Paderewski.

On this last visit to the United States, the great Pole was over seventy-five years old. He had come to mend his fortunes. He had lost everything in the war and was literally a poor man. His voice was still strong, but his hands trembled and shook so, he couldn't drink a glass of water without spilling half of it on his vest. At the piano his hands

Figure 25. Ignace Paderewski, c. 1920s. *Source*: Bain News Service, Library of Congress, Prints and Photographs Division.

were steady and his fingers fleet. When the waiter brought the bacon and eggs, Paderewski looked up at him, expecting to be recognized. The waiter returned his glance and asked: "Anything else, sir?"

"No," Paderewski replied and went on talking to me. When another couple sat down at the table opposite us, he again lifted his eyes, and seeing no glance of recognition, said: "Well, this is wonderful. I'm really not recognized," and he continued telling me what had happened in Poland and how he was not responsible for the anti-Semitic wave that engulfed his country while he was president. "I inherited the religious anti-Semitism inculcated into the people while the Russians had ruled Poland. Two hundred years of Russian miseducation could not be wiped out in a few years. I had been too optimistic. The Bolsheviks wiped out anti-Semitism in their country by wiping out the anti-Semites. I couldn't do that. I am a Pole. Stalin is a Georgian, not a Russian. A few million dead Russians meant nothing to him."

His tour had been marred by public demonstrations against him, and he was held responsible for conditions that were not in his power to remedy. He was too much the Polish patriot to defend himself, that he was not responsible for the barbarities, that such behavior was in the nature of the Polish people.

As breakfast continued, he looked up expectantly every time someone passed our table. By the time the coffee was brought, he asked in an irritable voice: "What kind of people come here, anyhow? This has never happened to me before. Here I've been for an hour, people have come and gone and not a sign of recognition. Have they never heard me play, heard of me or seen my picture in the papers and magazines?"

"Didn't you want a place where you wouldn't be bothered?" I asked.

"Yes, that's what I wanted," he admitted, and drank his coffee, but his brow was puckered and his face was flushed and there was a nervousness about his famous hands. Suddenly he put down his cup and said: "Let's go!"

On the way out he looked at the desk clerk and stopped to look at the doorman. Once outside, he exclaimed angrily: "This couldn't have happened anywhere else. Here I've been for two hours in a restaurant, and people were coming in and going out without recognizing me. Goodbye!" And he strode away.

When I met him again in Paris, a year or two later, he was still resentful about our breakfast. To soften the blow, I told him that he had been recognized, but that the people, at my request, had respected his desire for privacy; that the Algonquin was a place where many famous people came daily, just because nobody made a fuss over them. "Who, for instance?" he wanted to know. "What famous people come there?"

I enumerated the names of a few musicians: Godowsky, Elman, Bauer.

"Who would want autographs from them? Since when are they famous, and for what? Godowsky, yes. But not the others." He rebelled at the thought that I was putting him in the same class with the musicians whose names I had mentioned.

When I returned to my hotel on the Boulevard Raspail, I was told that Monsieur Paderewski had phoned. I returned the call. "I'm sorry," he told me. "I didn't mean to slight your friends, they are all wonderful people. I'm just a temperamental old man. Please do not hold my bad moods against me. Come for lunch. You must come. I'll play for you."

I promised. I pretended that his promise to play was irresistible. I never heard him play so poorly. When he stopped playing, he said: "My hands just won't behave today. Don't tell me I played well. I didn't."

∽

Harold Bauer, my favorite Mozart and Schumann player, and a man with a highly developed sense of humor, came down from the Beethoven Association one day and sat at my table, laughing at the top of his voice. Robert Nathan and I stared at him, knowing an amusing story would follow. "Do you know that Vladimir de Pachmann is here?"

Yes, we had heard about it. There was always something in the papers about de Pachmann, and not always about his latest concert. Though he was not only a great pianist, but an exciting one, his eccentricities attracted

Figure 26. Harold Bauer. *Source*: Library of Congress, Prints and Photographs Division.

more attention than his playing. It was not unusual for him to come out on the stage at Carnegie Hall, when it was filled to capacity, then turn around and return to the wings because his entrance was not as he had wished it. "A bad entrance," he would announce to the audience.

Pianists are still undecided as to whether de Pachmann's eccentricities were genuine or deliberate showmanship: to make people talk about him. He affected clerical garb and pretended that the cassock he wore at concerts had been given him by Franz Liszt. But there was little in de Pachmann that was religious, and in this he was not different from Liszt, who left many illegitimate children behind him.

Meeting his ex-wife at a party, he cried out at the top of his voice, pointing to her husband, Labori, the famous lawyer: "Why did you leave me to marry that oaf? Come back to your Vladimir, you still love him!"

Figure 27. Vladimir de Pachmann, c. 1918. *Source*: Library of Congress, Prints and Photographs Division.

The story had wings. The next day the concert hall was packed. "What brought you here?" de Pachmann asked from the stage. "The story about me and my former wife, or my playing?"

At other times he would sit at the piano, turn to the audience and, rubbing his little hands, would say to some lady in the first row: "I don't like your hat. Remove it. I won't play a note until you remove it." He would begin to play, then stop suddenly and announce that he would try it again, because he hadn't done it right the first time. Or he would stop after a brilliant passage, turn, and tell his audience that no one could play it as well, "not even Godowsky" he would shout, pointing to the box in which Godowsky sat. "He comes closer to it than anybody, but admit, Leopold, that even you can't do this as well!" After a few more eccentric displays, he would settle down to his program and play like a god.

Excepting Godowsky, de Pachmann had contempt for all pianists and pretended to be in fear of his life because they all, so he said, wanted to do away with him. He had waiters taste his food before he ate it, fearing that Paderewski had bribed the cook to poison him. When de Pachmann was in town, the columnists had lively stuff to report.

"And now," Bauer told us, "he is ill, and has canceled several concerts." Bauer continued, "Godowsky called to tell me that de Pachmann is ill. He'd been to see him every day, but now he had to go to Rochester to see his son, and asked me to visit his friend during his absence. I argued with Godowsky: de Pachmann doesn't like pianists and, consequently, doesn't like me. But Godowsky insisted: de Pachmann is a colleague, he is ill, he is a great pianist, he mustn't be left alone. Go. Stay with him for an hour. He is a very sick man.

"When I rang up de Pachmann's suite at the hotel, his secretary told me the master would be happy to see me. When I appeared, the secretary excused himself, went to the sick room and came out to say that the master would be ready to see me soon. A quarter of an hour later, the secretary ushered me into the room, and there was de Pachmann, lying in the bed with a black satin coverlet over him, his little white hands folded over it. He looked very ill. Very ill. His little waxen face wasn't bigger than my fist. His eyes were deep in their sockets.

"'Sit down, young man,' he greeted me, staring at the ceiling. 'What is your name?' Harold Bauer, the pianist, I told him. Godowsky asked me to come and see you. 'Oh, Bauer,' he said. 'I think I have heard the name. A German name. It means peasant. It also means bricklayer. It has many meanings in German.' Then, still talking at the ceiling, he launched into a story about Franz Liszt. People who haven't heard Liszt don't know what can be done on the piano. He had heard Liszt play. Had Godowsky also heard Liszt, he would have become a great pianist. At the end of about thirty minutes of this, during which I hadn't uttered a word, I looked at my watch and said that I was sorry, I had to leave.

"'Come again,' de Pachmann urged. 'This was the most brilliant conversation I've heard in a long time. Please come again. Why haven't you come before? Didn't you know I was ill?'

"'I knew, but I didn't come because I know you don't like pianists.'

"'Oh,' de Pachmann exclaimed, looking at me for the first time. 'Then YOU may come.'"

~

Speaking of round tables, there was another famous table long before the one at the Algonquin came into being. It was the oval table at Joel's on Forty-First Street near Seventh Avenue. Joel's was on three levels: the ground floor was a rather gaudy saloon-restaurant serving a free lunch just like any other saloon in those days, where one could see, at any time of the day, intellectual, mysterious, slick, well-dressed, and pugnacious Latin Americans, as well as a few more mysterious well-known American gunrunners.

Many South American revolutions were hatched there. Some of the men who had frequented Joel's place later became the dictators of their respective countries, and some of them lived long enough to come back to Joel's when a fresh revolution had displaced them. Others were not so lucky. South American revolutions were lethal to a succession of dictators. Some came back and wrote a book or two denouncing the new incumbent and were imprisoned by the American authorities for libeling the head of a friendly power. This happened to Carlo Fornaro, the author and painter, who wrote a book titled *Diaz, Czar of Mexico*. The word "czar" in those days was an insult. It didn't have the connotation it got later when we elevated people to be the czars of the motion picture industry, the garment industry, and the oil industry.

Joel's guests all called themselves revolutionaries, which they were, if one gives the word its broadest meaning. Hitler, too, was a revolutionist. South America grew and developed through a series of internal convulsions called uprisings, or revolutions, as one pleased, or depending on who was in the saddle and who called the names.

Figure 28. The Literary Table at Joel's Bohemia (New York), c. 1911, showing Joel Rinaldo, Michael Monahan, Leonard Charles van Noppen, Edwin Markham, Booth Tarkington, Benjamin de Casseres, and S. Osheel, caricature by Carlo de Fornaro. *Source*: Carlo de Fornaro, *Mortals & Immortals: Caricatures by C. de Fornaro* (New York: The Hornet Publishing Company, 1911), 41. Public domain.

The floor above the one on the street was given to what was one of the first night clubs in New York: a night club that was very different from the night clubs of today. That floor was not open to patrons until dinner time. At the far end of the long room was a large, oval table on which was a sign: THIS TABLE IS RESERVED FOR LITERARY PEOPLE, ARTISTS, AND THEIR FRIENDS. All about that section of the wall were drawings and caricatures of the men and women allowed at that table.

When one of the accredited habitués brought a friend who was accepted by the rest of the crowd, one of the artists drew a head of him, gave it to the waiter to have it framed, and it was soon on the wall. Todd Powers, Boardman Robinson, Courtney Lemon, Andre Tridon, Benjamin de Casseres, Harry Kemp, Eugene O'Neill, and a few other luminaries of these days, among them one or another of the Millay sisters, were nightly diners at that table. The price of drinks and food served to the artists was just half of what the other patrons were charged. Artists didn't mingle with the other guests, but occasionally one of the fraternity, in his cups, would approach some suburbanites to orate and expound some ultra-revolutionary literary, artistic, or philosophical theory, not out of any desire to convert or convince anybody, but to show his contempt for them. "Yokels. Who of you has ever read Walt Whitman? Can you tell me whether Balzac was a singer or a prize fighter?"

Harry Kemp, the tramp poet, was more frequently guilty of such behavior than anybody else. Hippolyte Havel, the anarchist writer and editor of *Mother Earth*, ran him a close second. His vocabulary was Homeric. When a patron objected, he was always wrong, and waiters had strict orders never to interfere with the artists. If one of them felt like interrupting a singer whose performance he didn't like, or stopping the orchestra and ordering them to play something else, he was free to do so. Havel, a Chicago-born Czech with a Gypsy strain in his blood, loved to dance on the table. Nobody ever stopped him.

Benjamin de Casseres, who claimed the distinction of being a descendant of Baruch Spinoza, and who started his literary career as a highbrow poet with a volume entitled *Fire-Eaters* and wound up as a columnist on one of Hearst's papers, was really the stormy petrel of Joel's. Joel Rinaldo, the owner of the place, worshipped Ben. In Joel's eyes, Ben was the greatest man that ever lived. Ben had traveled extensively and luxuriously all over Mexico with Fornaro at Joel's expense, and could have had everything he wanted from him. When Ben didn't like the people at a certain table, he would ask that they be thrown out. And thrown out they were, regardless of the costly champagne they had consumed. Joel never argued against any of Ben's decisions; for wasn't he a great poet and a lineal descendant of Spinoza? The truth, which Joel didn't know, was that Baruch Spinoza died childless; that if Ben did belong to the Spinoza family, it was through Baruch's sister, who had persecuted the philosopher.

At about one or two o'clock in the morning, Joel himself would occasionally sit down at the artist's table. The price for that privilege was to pay for all the drinks and food consumed until he had appeared and, of course, all that was consumed afterwards: nothing but the best—caviar and champagne. If one liked a singer and wanted her to come over and sing exclusively for the table, she was withdrawn from the floor and brought to sing for the artists. On the floor above was Joel's apartment, in which a few rooms were reserved for those of the fraternity who had drunk themselves too sick to go home.

Joel Rinaldo was an interesting figure: tall, very blonde, wearing his hair rather long, immaculately dressed, he looked more like an international diplomat than a saloon keeper. He appeared nightly at about ten o'clock and ambled about from the ground floor to the top floor and back, stopping at a table here and there and winding up at the oval table to discuss some point of philosophy, seemingly completely oblivious of the dancers, singers, customers, orchestra, and the capers cut by some of the patrons.

In addition to being the owner of the place, Joel had literary and philosophic pretensions. He had written a book on spontaneous generation which he had published himself and which was being peddled by the cigarette girls from table to table every night. Joel was happy when more of his books were sold one night than on the previous one. He attributed the sales, not to the selling ability of the girls, but to the growing interest in the subject, and would sit down at a buyer's table and order champagne on the house for the privilege of discussing the book: "I run this saloon to sell my books; to get my books across." It cost him ten dollars to sell a book for one dollar. Of course, nobody at the oval table believed in spontaneous generation, and no one hesitated to say so to Joel Rinaldo. That was their right. They were artists.

I remember one night when Leon Trotsky, then residing in the Bronx, was one of the guests, brought there by Hippolyte Havel. Trotsky, of course, wanted to talk about the coming Russian revolution, but Joel, seeing a new face, wanted to talk about spontaneous generation and argued that even the revolution in Russia contradicted old academic science. Joel could tie up his theory with everything: art, politics, literature, music, and science. Trotsky was a very suave gentleman when he wasn't in the saddle. He didn't contradict Joel. He listened quietly and attentively and smiled. He was an erudite man. There isn't another one like him in the Russia of today. His *History of the Russian Revolution* is as revealing as that of Stalin is confusing.

Later, under the influence of Andre Tridon, one of the first psychoanalysts in America, a man of much unhealthy talent who often quoted Freud as his authority though no one could find the quotation he referred to, Joel wrote a book on psychoanalysis. Andre, no doubt, had helped with that book. Joel, with a new subject, was so wrapped up in it, he would sit down at a stranger's table, interrupt the program if the orchestra disturbed him, and talk about psychoanalysis, about libidos and complexes: new words in the language. Later on Joel discovered Rabelais, by osmosis with a Rabelaisian self-styled authority, and there was no stopping him.

This went on for many years, while many revolutions were being hatched on the ground floor and many men slept off their drunkenness on the third floor. And then suddenly, without warning, Joel got married, closed the joint, moved to an immense house in Brooklyn with a tremendous library, a bar stocked with the most expensive liquors, and invited his best and oldest friends to visit him: drinks free, food free, as long as they talked and listened: "Come one, come all. I love the human voice."

He had become a middle-class, bourgeois, retired gentleman with a keen interest in everything, but a complete detachment from the things to which he had been formerly attached. South American revolutions continued to be hatched elsewhere, around Columbus Circle, but Joel would no longer have anything to do with them. He now appears at the Algonquin several times a year to see what's going on: "I want to see whether some of the people I knew years ago are still alive, how they look, how they act, how some of them bear up under prosperity, how well they carry their fame on their shoulders. I am just curious."

"How about Ben? Do you see Ben often?"

"Ben? Oh . . . him. No."

I saw Joel after Ben's death. He didn't even mention the fact.

～

There were, and still are, other round tables elsewhere. There was a round table at Jack's, on Sixth Avenue between Forty-First and Forty-Second Streets, to which the elite of the theatre used to repair after midnight for steak and beer. Intellectual discussions at that table were as rare as hen's teeth, but it did have a certain reputation. People whose names had just gone up in lights, or whose plays were produced, felt it incumbent upon them to be seen at Jack's, even if for nothing other than to show off the ladies they escorted. After all, prosperity is a mark of success. One cannot carry one's bank book on one's shirtfront, but a bejeweled lady on one's arm is something no failure can afford. The steaks at Jack's were large and expensive.

There is another round table at the Café Royal, on Twelfth Street and Second Avenue. As a matter of fact, there are many round tables there. It is the meeting ground for all the Jewish, Hungarian, German, Romanian, and Russian writers, actors, playwrights, producers, directors, newspaperman, chorus girls, and artists. Jack London used to dine there frequently, and so did John Reed, poet, writer, traveler, one of the first American communists. Reed died in Russia and was buried underneath the Kremlin. He was one of the most romantic figures in American journalism. Poet, playwright, athlete, he was up-front on every liberal cause. The spectacular manifestation he had organized at Madison Square Garden to raise funds for the Paterson silk mill strikers will never be forgotten. Had he lived, he would have been the first to denounce what he once believed to be the hope of the world, communism. From time to time, Eugene O'Neill, Max Eastman, and a few other early rebels were seen there. They found the international atmosphere invigorating. Every fresh wind blowing something new in modern literature and art made its first appearance at the Café Royal. Existentialism was an old story on Second Avenue by the time the name became known to Broadway.

The Café Royal is still there, still as interesting as ever, and many Algonquinites are often seen at its tables. International actors and actresses are hired there, contracts for foreign plays are decided by a handshake before two witnesses, over a glass of tea. It is via the Café Royal on Second Avenue that Paul Muni, Jacob Ben Ami, Stella Adler, Luther Adler, Alla Nazimova, Bertha Kalisch, Clifford Odets, and a large number of other eminences in the American theatre emerged. The late Jacob Adler, father of all the Adlers on the American stage and in the movies: six feet, four inches tall, never without a silk hat on his beautiful head, ascot tie, and gold-handled cane, used to make his entrance at midnight every night, after the show, followed by a group of hangers-on who never let him out of their sight, and who were nicknamed "the patriots." Jacob Adler was the Pied Piper. His fans numbered tens of thousands. Every inch an actor, he was one of the handsomest men I have seen anywhere and had the demeanor of a king. He was a sucker for plays in which he played the role of a king. His King Lear is unsurpassed.

Stella Adler, his gorgeous daughter, a frequent Algonquinite, still comes to the Royal, and often, after looking around, remarks: "To think that these nonentities sit on the same chairs on which papa used to sit." Stella offered to take Menachem Begin, the leader of the Irgun, the underground army of Israel, to the Royal one night, when he was in

Figure 29. Jacob Adler in *The Merchant of Venice*, c. 1903. *Source*: Folger Shakespeare Library, Creative Commons Attribution-ShareAlike 4.0 International License (CC BY-SA 4.0).

New York. Begin was so tired he fell asleep on my shoulder in the car, so I told the chauffeur to drive to the hotel instead. What Stella hadn't told me was that she had prepared a huge reception there for her hero.

It would be difficult to explain why the Café Royal attracts all these people. As a business, it has been sold so many times, no one knows anymore who the owner is. The last owner was a former waiter in the place, about whom a successful play was written: *Café Royal*, which starred Sam Jaffe, and had quite a run on Broadway. Before the Royal became a literary center, the same people used to meet at Stahl's Café, a dozen blocks further south, and before that they congregated in a café on East Broadway, owned by a man who was reputed to know the texts of fifty plays by heart and eager to display his knowledge:

"Sholem, let's hear the second scene of the third act of *King Lear*."

"Just a moment: let me give this customer his change, first."

Why they moved away from there and why they now herd together at the Royal no one can tell. In itself, the Royal has no atmosphere and no attempt was made to create one. Inside and out, it looks like many another cafés in the neighborhood.

~

Some years ago, the Algonquin came very close to losing its attractiveness by a faux pas made by one of its managers. In bad humor, he approached one of the tables at which a group of young men sat and said: "You talk too loud. This is not a synagogue."

Without a word, the young men left. Once outside, they called up some of the habitués of the Round Table and reported what had been said to them. The next day, the manager's words, somewhat garbled, appeared in a newspaper. At lunch that same day, the Round Table was deserted, and many other tables were vacant. And then Frank woke up to what was happening. It was solely due to the charm in which he wrapped his explanations and worded his apologies that the Round Table habitués came back, though in the meantime some of the others had gone to other restaurants to make their headquarters there to this day, with an occasional look in on Forty-Fourth Street. Atmosphere is, indeed, a fragile vessel, more so than the most fragile china.

During the summer months, many New Yorkers disappear from the city to go out of town for their vacation, but their places are taken by people who come from all over the country to spend their vacation in New York. The uninitiated do not realize what a vacation town New York is. In July, thousands of school teachers from the South and the West come to spend a few months in the big city.

For nine months of the year, they map out the places they want to visit: the Metropolitan Museum of Art, the Museum of Natural History, Radio City, and, if they have a literary or romantic bent, the Algonquin. In July, August, and September, the hotel and dining rooms are taken over by the vacationists, who center all their admiration on the few celebrities left in town. A successful musical comedy, a new play, a boxing match, fills the Algonquin to overflowing with tourists. Samuel Hoffenstein, the poet, came to the Algonquin every day during the summer: "To have all the admiration centered on myself," he explained.

~

Immediately after World War I, when the nickelodeon was already a memory and the advent of the war had brought about the twenty-five-cent seat, the motion picture producers, no longer able to make pictures "off the cuff," improvising as they went along, finally came to the conclusion that they had to hire professional writers to write the motion picture stories and titles. Until then, everybody, anybody, wrote stories and scripts for pictures.

The titles of those early silent pictures were inane and frequently had no relation at all to the scene shown on the screen. Most of the movie producers, former industrialists, sold on specialization, hired one writer for the story, one for the script, and a third for the titles. Eventually these writers gained or lost reputations as story writers, script writers, and title writers, but once hired for one specialty, they were stuck with it for good. To this day, this specialization holds sway. So and so is the best treatment man, so and so the best script man, and so and so's dialog is unsurpassed. Most scenarios are built on the garment plan: one is a sleeve-maker, the other a pocket-maker. There are very few writers allowed to do a story for the screen from beginning to end. That is why so many motion pictures are lopsided and so badly dovetailed. Writers who have become producers have tried to break away from the carry-over tradition, but are held back by the powers that be.

Speaking of specialization, the story is told of a young physician visiting an old practitioner. "Are you going to be in general practice?" the older man asked.

"No. I intend to specialize."

"The stomach?"

"No."

"Nose, ear, and throat?"

"No. Only the nose."

"Which nostril?" the old doctor asked.

~

The Algonquin became a sort of hiring hall, and producers and agents swooped down from California to pick the best of the crop. Not being familiar with writers and their work, they, of course, consulted Case, who advised something in the interest of the company and sometimes to get rid of some bore he didn't like, or to help out a writer in distress. Out of one of these swoops, an agent carried away two schoolteachers on vacation Case had recommended. Put to work title-writing, they have since become completely engulfed in the motion picture business, following it in all its phases. Thus two schoolteachers were lost. So were some hotel bellboys, waiters, ad writers, publicity agents, dentists, and doctors. It was not so long ago that a man who had written a book and given it a maritime title—though the story had nothing of the sea in it—was brought to Hollywood to sit in as an expert during the making of a sea picture. He is still a sea expert, a high-priced authority, although when first hired he didn't know the pup from the prow.

Hollywood was a crude town, the motion picture industry was in a crude condition, and the arrival of real writers on motion picture lots bewildered the studio magnates and their assistants. Clayton Hamilton, a professor of dramatics at Columbia University, was one of the first of the "learned" men weaned away from a college to the fleshpots of Hollywood; he was hired by a mogul to write titles. That particular producer, of whom Chaplin once said, "he knows what he wants but can't spell it," had made the discovery during a slump in the motion-picture business that people who paid fifty cents to see a picture wanted "literary" titles. However, when a picture titled by Clayton Hamilton was shown in the projection room of the studio, this same producer leaned over to his assistant and asked: "What is there in these titles to show that a $30,000 a year man wrote them? The office boy could have done the same job. Why didn't he put in a few big words to show that a learned man wrote the titles? 'Perpendicular,' for instance. A word like that shows something that it wasn't written by the office boy." God knows where he had heard the word: possibly from his son, studying elementary geometry. He insisted that the word "perpendicular" be in one or two of the titles, to prove it was written by a $30,000 a year man. And it was. Every once in a while a producer would come upon a big word and demand a place for it in one of his pictures: Perpendicular. Horizontal. Dimensional. Enzymatic. Progressive. Encyclopedic.

On another occasion on another lot, where another learned man was hired to write titles, the producer looked at the rushes of a picture, in which a young man was pleading with his lady love, asking her to wait for him; that he was going off to Mexico to make his fortune in oil and would soon come back for her.

"Oh John, you are an optimist," the title read.

"Why don't you use words plain people will understand?" the producer asked the writer. "Now, you and I know that an optimist is an eye doctor, but does the public know it?"

It was in this intellectual atmosphere that some of the writers were called upon to work. Many of them, sick of parties, drink, and the wilds of Vine Street, having done their stint, cashed their last checks and drove back to New York, vowing never again to return to Hollywood. But they did, because of the fleshpots, and because in Hollywood they didn't have to work too hard to get the lucre. Publishers weren't as generous as producers. In Hollywood, writers had enough leisure to play golf every day, write novels, short stories, and plays. The opinion, false or true, that motion picture work destroyed literary ability hadn't yet gained general currency with editors and publishers. Today, any writer who has cultivated the gardens of Allah and manured the flowerbeds of Beverly Hills has two strikes against him when he offers a play or a story to a publisher.

The continual traffic between California and New York reached a new high when some of the name actors who had shied away from the movies, considering them a step down in the profession, relented and followed the lure of the silver screen. A contract with the movies is no longer denounced as an act of prostitution, but as a goal to be achieved. Although few could, all our great stage lovers were competing with Rudolph Valentino. An actor, however, has a hell of a time reestablishing himself when he comes back to New York to act in a play. Critics are a suspicious lot. You'll often read: "Mr. B. has become too glib. What he says sounds hollow. If he wants to come back to the stage, he'll have to forget the screen."

~

Having trained his staff to take care of all the details, as the Algonquin became prosperous, Case became an assiduous traveler between New York and Hollywood. He had many friends on the West Coast, among whom the closest were the Fairbankses, Doug and Mary, who made his hotel their home whenever they were in New York and were friends of the family. By that time, many of the Round Table of the Rose Room were serving time in Hollywood: Joe Mankiewicz, Charles Brackett, Nunnally Johnson, Robert Sherwood, Bob Benchley, and quite a few luminaries from other tables. An empty chair in the dining room, vacated by an old friend, would send Case packing and off to California in a few hours: "I am going to visit my friends in the money penitentiary."

Whenever Frank Case arrived in Hollywood, Algonquinites gathered about him like exiles gathering about a newcomer from their beloved country. They dined and wined him and plied him with questions. It gave

Figure 30. Bercovici, Mary Pickford, Charlie Chaplin, and Douglas Fairbanks at Charlie Chaplin Studios back lot, where Bercovici had a bungalow/office, c. 1920s. *Source*: Mirana Comstock.

Frank the sense of importance he craved when he was among people of the pen and stage: "I have written two books. But am I a hotel keeper who writes books, or a book writer who owns a hotel?"

What was more natural than for Frank to begin to think about building an Algonquin in Hollywood? It was the era of expansion. There were many hotel chains. Case had a vision of an Algonquin chain, one in Hollywood, another in Chicago, another one in New Orleans. "And that was only the beginning," as Mark Twain's Colonel Sellers said. An Algonquin in Paris and London: for the expatriates. There were, of course, hotels and restaurants in Movieland scattered from Vine Street to Beverly Hills where the fraternity gathered: the two Brown Derbys, Levi's, Musso Frank, Chassen's, Lucy's, Victor Hugo, and, of course, Henry Bergman's place on Hollywood Boulevard. You no doubt remember Henry, the fat man in Chaplin's early pictures. Chaplin, who had a poverty complex, financed Bergman's restaurant to make sure he'll never go hungry. As an adjunct to the restaurant, Henry owned a farm on which he raised thousands of chickens and milked two score cows.

The idea of a Hollywood Algonquin appealed to the Fairbankses and to a number of others who were willing and ready to back it to the hilt financially. While the heat was on, they picked a site, bought it, and paid a fantastic price for the property. In the meantime, Frank was called back to New York on business. Leaving the tale about the forthcoming enterprise to take root in California, he spread the news in New York, telling writers and actors that he was building a home for them there. Hollywood with an Algonquin would become a paradise. The new Athens, the center of all the arts, would no longer be without an Academy. "The motion picture will eventually replace the written word and stage play. Get in on the ground floor, boys and girls." The displacement of the written word was the dream of the illiterates. They who had never read a book were tired of reading.

The plans progressed rapidly. On Frank's subsequent trip to California, everything was ready but the laying of the cornerstone. I can just about imagine the hullabaloo around such an affair. The music, speeches, the big lights playing on the stars, immortalizing the golden shovels with ivory inlaid handles as they dug the emplacement of the cornerstone; not an ordinary cornerstone, but one chiseled out by a famous sculptor, a specialist in chiseled cornerstones, and with all the names engraved on it, for the archaeologists, a thousand or two years later.

At a gathering of his friends, Frank was asked to expound on his plans for a few new stockholders who hadn't yet heard them. Briefly said, he only intended to bring the mountain to Mohammed. Everybody agreed it would be a good thing and promised support. However, Arthur Byron shook his leonine head: "No. It cannot be. We stay here for months, working, but thinking that when it's over we'll leave, go back where we came from; to New York, to act on the stage, to write books, plays. We go to Forty-Fourth Street and see our friends and breathe some uncontaminated air and talk to people about other things than motion pictures. It's good to talk about motion pictures, but it is very bad to talk about motion pictures only. I want to see real people, not shadows. Hear voices, real voices, as they are used in life. An Algonquin in Hollywood would be nothing but an imitation, and all imitations are desecrations. I want the real thing. I don't want to be fooled into staying here any longer than I have to, longer than I care to. I am an exile. I don't even want to consider Hollywood as my permanent residence.

"It's a wonderful place, and beautiful, too; and it has been good to me, to us: it has permitted us to expand our influence. It is a roof over my head, but my home is elsewhere." Becoming more eloquent, he pleaded: "Who are we, all of us, here? Prisoners of the dollar. Don't most of us expect to escape? Of course, some of us have waited a long time," and he looked at Samuel Hoffenstein, the poet whose volume *Poems About Practically Nothing* had been one of the first best sellers among books of poetry.

He didn't have to tell Hoffenstein's story. Everybody knew it. Sam had left New York for Hollywood several years before, to write the treatment for a screenplay. I believe it was Theodore Dreiser's *An American Tragedy*, on a year's contract at a salary of $15,000. It was five times more than Sam had ever earned. And so he had figured that at the end of the year, having spent $3,000, he would have enough money to come back to New York and live for four years and write the kind of poetry he had always wanted to write, even if it didn't bring in a cent. Sam was on the way to becoming to American poetry what Heinrich Heine had been to German poetry. He was one of the few mortals who knew how to blend the lyrical wine with the juice of irony and make both taste the better for the mixture. But he had spent three times as much that year as he had intended, and his tastes had become somewhat more expensive, so he figured it would be best to stay another year and accumulate some more money, to live a little better in New York than one could live on $3,000 a year.

But the following year, his taste having become more expensive, he found himself with no economies at all. He couldn't live as cheaply as he had once lived in New York. People in Hollywood just had to live up to their salaries. He was invited to parties given by other writers and had to return the compliment. And parties were expensive affairs. Since his salary had been increased to $20,000 a year, he might save half of that, he figured: in two years he would have $20,000 in the bank, and then he would go back to New York and write in the luxury of leisure. But Sam stayed in Hollywood twenty years. His salary rose eventually to $3,000 a week, but he never accumulated enough money to permit him to take off enough time to write poetry; a leisure he had only during his last illness, during which he completed a book of poetry that was published on the day of his death. And that book wasn't half as good as the first one. It was its inferior by twenty years.

Byron's cry, that building an Algonquin in Hollywood would rob some of the old Algonquinites of an illusion, while giving them a poor imitation, had its effect. People began to shake their heads and turned lukewarm to the project. Frank himself saw Byron's point. Though he had a great time whenever he came to Hollywood and was flattered to be one of the constant guests at Pickfair, where he met the great and famous on equal terms, he realized that he couldn't dance at two parties at the same time; that, in the end, he too would prefer to see his friends on their rare visits in New York than to see them permanently established in Hollywood. Whenever the spirit moved him, he was well enough supplied with cash to go there and be a guest instead of a host. The plan for a Hollywood Algonquin was abandoned. The New York hotel continued as the hiring hall and the excuse for producers and agents to take a trip to New York to see some of the new plays. The stage play wasn't dying. It still supplies the movies with the best subjects they distort.

In due time, many of the exiles, having brought their families to California or married in the picture industry, established themselves permanently and took root there; particularly those who had children. Though some of them had become proficient in the new medium and became wealthy, few of the more talented ones ever produced anything worthwhile in literature after working in the motion picture industry a certain length of time. Occasionally, one of them attempts to tear themselves away from the gilded cage and return to their first love, but the savory odor of the fleshpots brings them back to Movieland. When they first come to New York, they vow never to return to Hollywood. After a few months in the big city, during which they try to recall the Muse, and only meet with suspicion by publishers, editors, and theatrical producers, they generally return to Beverly Hills and vow never to return to New York. But they do, again and again, and again and again they ask for the same room in the Algonquin in which they had done their best work years and years ago.

"What's the matter? You changed the color of the walls. There was a different sofa in this room. Can't I have back my chair? Where is Georges? Is Nick still here?"

"Hello, Miss Bush. I'm home again. I want Nick to serve my break-fast. Papa Mitchell still here? Oh, it's his day off. Tell him I am here."

The tale is told of a writer who years ago brought his family to Hollywood after his play had failed in New York. Anyone who had a play produced on Broadway, even a failure, stood a better chance of employment in the movies than a novelist whose book was a best seller. A very adaptable person, the gentleman in question rose high in the motion picture industry and soon lived in an expensive mansion, with a swimming pool, chauffeur, several cars, a butler, cook, house servants, and a private secretary. As is customary among the high-salaried in the motion picture capital, his children went to an expensive private school, where they met children of other similarly high-salaried parents. Children of $5,000-a-week parents don't chum with children of $3,000-a-week papas.

The week before Christmas, the teacher proposed to the pupils that they each write a composition about the lives of poor people. The next day little Walter, the son of the writer, brought an original composition to school that read: "There once was a papa and a mama who were very poor. Terribly poor. So poor they didn't have anything to eat, and didn't have any clothes. And their chauffeur was poor and their butler was poor and their cook was poor."

Every one of this gilded-cage youth has several tutors: a tutor for dancing, another for physical training; a tutor for piano playing and a tutor for French. One day a little girl, after watching a boy climb a tree agilely, asked: "Will you give me the name and address of your tutor in tree climbing? I'll have Father get him for me."

$\sim$

Alexander Woollcott, after many of his friends had departed for greener pastures, used to come to the entrance of the Rose Room and, after a quick look around at the crowd, tell Georges: "There is nobody here." Then he would leave.

Georges, somewhat of a psychologist, thought Woollcott came especially when he knew his friends were not at their accustomed place, just so as to ignore a room crowded with people. Woollcott was a beau mot specialist, forever in search of an occasion to place them.

$\sim$

Mr. Ben B. Bodne, the present host of the Algonquin, tells the following story: "One morning, Mrs. Bodne came down to the lobby and said: 'There is a man sitting on the floor of the hallway in front of Mr. Laughton's suite.'

"'Do you know who he is?' I asked.

"She didn't know, so I rode up in the elevator to the Laughton suite. The man was still sitting there, leaning against the actor's door. It was Mr. ———, a novelist, who had been with us for many months; a quiet man, whom I had never known to drink. As a matter of fact, I hadn't ever seen him talk to anybody in the lobby or the dining room. 'Shhh,' he cautioned, pulling me down on the floor beside him when he saw me. 'Listen.'

"And so I listened. From behind the door came Laughton's booming voice, rehearsing the story of David and Goliath, which he was to broadcast that night. I was in an awkward position. What if any of the other guests passed by and saw me sitting there on the floor? I didn't relish that idea. It was a very awkward fix. I made several attempts to get up, but the man held me back and shushed me. And he wasn't drunk: 'Be quiet and listen!,' he whispered in my ear, 'Listen to the story.'

"Mr. Laughton repeated several of the passages in the Bible, trying to get the right tone, the right rhythm, the right intonation. When he finished, with David smiting Goliath between the eyes with a stone from his slingshot and striding over to sever the giant's head, the novelist rose, rather weak in the knees. I offered to see him to his room, just around the corner from Mr. Laughton's suite. He invited me in. There was not the faintest odor of liquor on his breath. He had seldom had visitors and was almost never seen at the bar. Looking around I could see his bed had not been slept in. There was a pile of paper on the table next to the typewriter. I called room service and asked Nick to bring up some coffee. The man looked unnerved as he paced up and down the room.

"'Is anything wrong?' I asked. 'I see you haven't slept all night.'

"'No, I haven't' he admitted and murmured under his breath, 'so David smote Goliath and then cut off his head, cut off his head, cut off his head.' By the time the coffee came, he had calmed down a little. 'You must think I'm crazy,' he said, 'sitting there on the floor against Mr. Laughton's door. But I worked all night to finish the book I started two years ago. I was just going down for coffee when I heard Mr. Laughton's voice. At first I couldn't hear what he said, but the rhythm was familiar, so I stood there and listened. Soon I knew it was the story of David and Goliath. I've worked a whole year, writing the story of David and Goliath without knowing it. My novel is about a little man triumphing over a giant; little David, going out to conquer Goliath, the giant public. But will he smite it between the eyes? That's the question! But how that man can read a story! How he uses his voice to milk the meaning out of every, every word!'"

Mr. Bodne, I am almost certain, could not have appreciated a similar situation three years ago, when he first came to the Algonquin. Three years have wrought a considerable change in his attitude and his understanding of the unusual people housed under his roof. He not only understood the man but appreciated the tension and the despair that followed the completion of the book.

An artist, whether a writer, painter, musician or actor, begins their work with great confidence and a certainty that they will be able to transmit their dream, their idea, on paper, on canvas, or in musical sound. Having thought about it for months, if not years, they begin to carry out their plan only when they feel it is ripe within them. If the work can be completed during the white heat of first inspiration, it leaves a wonderful feeling. But when it takes a longer time, the fires are soon lowered, and the artist has to keep on feeding the furnace within them with all the ingenuity and technique acquired in the years gone by. An artist's genius conceives what their talent has to carry through. By the time the work is half-finished, they have partly consumed themselves. Towards the end of the work they have lost most, if not all, perspective on what they have produced. They no longer know whether what they have done is what they originally wanted to do.

It frequently happens that an artist starts out to do one thing and that the characters of their play or novel, the figures on their canvas, take on a life of their own, and, instead of being directed by, direct the hand of their creator. Minor characters often take the bit between their teeth and run away with the whole show. A comedy becomes a tragedy and vice versa. It happens that a play or a novel turns out all the better for having taken a different direction then the one intended. When that happens, the artist is left with a feeling of defeat, with the feeling of a leader who has been led astray: to better pastures, but astray. And since every creation depends on the approval of many before it sees the light of day—the editor, publisher, producer, director, and afterwards depends on the approval of the public—doubt and despair set in powerfully before the last stroke is brushed on the canvas or the last word is pounded out on the typewriter.

Sit in the lobby of the Algonquin and watch the faces of many of its guests. One man comes down the elevator with some definite intention, but it has left him before he sets a foot out of the elevator and he stands there, trying to recall why he has come down. He may suddenly go back on the next elevator, hoping to find in his room the reason for coming down, as if he had lost it there. Of course, artists are forgetful. The only things they don't forget are praise and adverse criticism.

You may see a man or a woman rush down to ask the headwaiter whether the person with whom he or she had an appointment had arrived, or rush to see whether the expected letter is in the mail, and then walk out into the street in bedroom slippers. Another one goes to a table to sit down for lunch with friends and talks and laughs with them. Suddenly there is a vague look in his eyes. A new idea has just struck him; something to be added to a story he is writing, or to be taken out of it. Afraid that the idea will vanish before he pins it down on paper, he excuses himself and runs up to his room. His friends may wait a long time for him to reappear, if he hasn't completely forgotten to do so.

Some writers get so inhibited, so blocked by a situation, they just wander about the lobby. They stand at the bar with a full glass—or many empty glasses—before them, looking about to find someone to talk to: the waiter, the bartender, the host, anyone, some distraction or entertainment, any excuse for not going back to work. Any psychologist will tell you of coming across writers whose hands became paralyzed when they tried to touch a pencil or go near a typewriter.

There are people in the arts who work in the same rhythm as they would in an office. They are manufacturers who have acquired a certain technique in writing, painting, or acting. They know no depressed feeling, no despair, no disappointment; but neither do they have the ecstasy of creative moments. Their work is always of an even fabric, depending chiefly on a clever or marketable idea which they have either invented or are using another person's idea from a different angle. There are quite a few of their kind and doing commercially quite well, thank you. They are always seen at the right places, in the right clothes, and with the right people. Their hands never go back on them at the sight of pen or typewriter. To listen to their talk of markets and trends and prices, one might think that they are talking about stocks and bonds. It is, no doubt, easier to get along with them than with creative artists, Algonquin waiters, managers, and telephone operators will tell you, but it is wrong to judge the others by their standards. The "others" are the unusual people. Ordinary standards cannot and should not be applied to them. It is not the manufacturer of plays and stories and novels who creates or lends atmosphere to the Forty-Fourth Street inn. There is a strange quality about the "others"; a certain vibration emanates from them wherever they are. Their mere presence fills a room.

Let William Faulkner, the Southern novelist, be in the dining room and the very walls suddenly acquire a mysterious quality. To look at him you'd wonder why. He is a short, dark, quiet little man of no striking appearance, but somehow all that he has thought, all that he has done, wraps him in an aura that follows him.

Henry James Furman hasn't done much of late, but his presence carries all he has done until now. You couldn't mistake him and his wife, a pianist of great ability, for ordinary people.

Let Dorothy Thompson be somewhere—anywhere—and that massive, beautiful head of hers erases all the other feminine heads beside her, while Hemingway, wherever he is, emanates a strong masculinity; as if he and his clothes were impregnated with the odor of musk and amber.

Ward Morehouse is the theatre, wherever he is.

The restlessness of Marc Connelly transmits itself to the whole Rose Room. People sitting behind him begin to fidget, even when they don't know who he is.

Figure 31. Dorothy Thompson, c. 1940. *Source*: Library of Congress, Prints and Photographs Division.

There was always a tremulous atmosphere about Alexander Woollcott. Despite his mustache, he looked like a huge cat, poised to pounce upon the first moving thing within the reach of his claws. His moods were in his eyes and on his lips, and expressed themselves in the trembling of his jelly-like, huge stomach.

Louis Nizer entering the lobby makes you feel that here is a man sure of himself; who knows that he won't be beaten in an argument. Frank Kingdon comes in and fills the Oak Room by his mere presence. Peggy Wood, lovely Peggy Wood, radiates serenity and sparkling wit at the same time.

When a half-dozen of these people are in one room, the air is surcharged with electricity, coursing in all directions at once. And yet few of them are loud-spoken or make conspicuous gestures, nor do they dress differently from other people.

~

Vilhjalmur Stefansson, the famous author and explorer, Fannie Hurst, and I were lunching one day in the Rose Room, just after Stefansson had received considerable publicity for his demonstration that a man could live on raw meat alone without suffering any dire consequences as a result of the diet. He and several other explorers had submitted themselves to the raw meat experiment under medical supervision. The others quit after a few days, not because they were losing weight or because their physical condition had become impaired, but because they were plagued by the memory of the taste of other foods. Stefansson was the only one who carried out the experiment to the end and proved his contention.

Arriving a few minutes late, I found that my hosts had already ordered their lunch.

Stefansson's lunch consisted of a sandwich of raw, warm, chopped steak, with a huge blanket of fresh caviar between the layers of meat. Fannie Hurst, an old friend of his, was not astonished at such a meal. My own stomach did a few somersaults at the sight of this carnivore's feast. However, the waiter acted as though he had served the same fare for years. He put the plate down on the table and went about his business without another look at it.

Stefansson looked amused when the waiter brought my lunch. He knew of my own exotic tastes in food, having occasionally met me at restaurants which specialized in such fare. "Ever eat such a sandwich?" he asked.

Figure 32. Vilhjalmur Stefansson, c. 1915. *Source*: Library of Congress, Prints and Photographs Division.

"No. Is this a demonstration for my benefit, or is it the kind of food you really prefer?"

"It's what he prefers," Fannie Hurst sighed.

"Another sandwich, Mr. Stefansson?" the waiter inquired, noncommittally.

"He has a sense of humor," Fannie said.

"No," Stefansson maintained. "He has probably tried one in the kitchen and found it to his taste."

During all this, Frank Case stood at the door and watched the great explorer. After a while he sat down at our table, but seeing a second sandwich approaching, he rose hastily and asked: "Do you think it advisable to add sandwich à la Stefansson to the menu?"

Raul, the headwaiter, tells that Peter Lorre, the actor, who drinks Rhine wine for breakfast instead of coffee, has taught him how to make a special dressing for his salad: with aspirin, saccharine, and mineral oil. So, don't wonder that Peter Lorre looks so, well . . . different isn't the exact word.

Bob Davis, the famous editor, columnist, and discoverer of O. Henry, was famous as a gourmet, too. Bob was literally charged with electricity. When you shook hands with him, a current passed through you. Standing on a woolen rug, one of my hands in his and the other on a brass doorknob, I suffered an electric shock that shook me from head to toe. Bob Davis often went to the kitchen to see that his food was prepared the way he liked it. He would stand over the stove, stopwatch in hand, when eggs were boiling, and insisted that they be boiled in a certain amount of water to which he added the exact amount of salt. "Only savages boil their eggs without a pinch of salt in the water," he maintained. The Algonquin chef laughed. Davis had to look at a piece of meat before it was broiled for him. When someone ordered the wrong wine, he left the table, not to witness the sacrilege.

Figure 33. Sinclair Lewis, 1914. *Source*: Library of Congress, Prints and Photographs Division.

Sinclair Lewis's ambition has always been to own a restaurant, and though his own tastes in food are nothing out of the ordinary, he loves kitchen odors well enough to either take a table close to the kitchen or to inspect it at lunch or dinner time. At one time he offered to buy a partnership in the Algonquin, to obtain control of the kitchen. Frank Case was on the verge of closing the deal when he shuddered at the thought of what might happen between a temperamental chef with a carving knife and Red with a pencil behind his ear. The hotel business, in general, had a great fascination for Lewis.

Sherwood Anderson would begin his meal with dessert and work backwards, to the soup. After soup he generally called for a salad, with special instructions as to how the dressing should be prepared: so much lemon juice and a pinch of brown sugar over the mustard. And he wouldn't eat the salad unless it was brought to him in a wooden bowl. "Anderson fills an empty room all by himself," Case used to say. He had read only one story by Anderson, "Hands," and quoted it to the author every time he saw him, until Anderson cried out one day: "Another Sherwood wrote that story!"

Melvyn Douglas, a lover of food, who looks like a young college president on his vacation, has to watch himself lest he appear plumper in the middle of a picture than he was at the beginning, but orders huge quantities of food at which he only pecks.

Some years ago, the two of us went on a two week's loaf together to San Francisco. For weeks beforehand, we had planned our meals. He had memories of certain restaurants in San Francisco where he would have eaten his fill had he had the money at the time. The son of a famous musician, he has inherited, besides a love for music, also the musician's appreciation for food. We made our first stop at Monterey, and there at the wharf we consumed so much seafood, people stood about us, wondering when we had eaten before. An Italian fisherman who had just brought in a bag of huge salmon, asked: "You two fellows been in jail a long time, or what?" When he recognized Melvyn, he insisted that we go to his house and eat one of his specialties; fish, crab, lobster, shrimp: the whole cooked slowly over a charcoal fire in an earthen pot filled with wine, garlic, and tomato sauce.

But that meal was only an hors d'oeuvre compared to our culinary debauches when we reached San Francisco. The waiter at the California Market remembered Melvyn from a previous excursion with another friend and greeted him with effusion. His eyes lit up. Then he asked, pointing at me: "Can he eat?" Receiving an affirmative, he went to the kitchen. We ate for three hours without stop.

For dinner, we went to another restaurant: not that there was anything wrong with the first one, but because we were ashamed to appear there again so soon. The next morning we had champagne with our eggs and for lunch wound up at the Rubayat, whose chef is world famous, and whose father had been a chef in the capital of my own native land. This, and the fact that he admired Melvyn and had read some of my stories, put him on his mettle. Francis Lederer, the actor, joined us when we were half through, and from then on we had to taste the most exquisite dishes prepared especially for us, and drink the appropriate wines with each one. When everything seemed to be over, one dessert followed another, the last one being prepared in rose petals steamed over Benedictine. It made our heads swim. I still don't know how Lederer went through his performance that night, but Melvyn and I bore up quite well and continued the food orgy that night.

When we returned to Los Angeles, Melvyn's picture had to be postponed for several weeks until he got rid of some of the avoirdupois he had acquired. He has, no doubt, been on a strict diet ever since and only satisfies his gourmet eyes when he sits down to eat. When we lunched at the Algonquin, while he played in *Two Blind Mice*, he didn't look a day older or a pound heavier. Poor Melvyn. "How lucky you are, not to be an actor," he said, and then talked about his war experiences in India.

The late Montague Glass, author of the Potash and Perlmutter stories, most of which were written in the suite I now occupy, was also interested in cooking and in food. He was a big man with a laughing face, who always managed to find somebody to talk to about food an hour before every meal, to work up an appetite. Monty knew every famous chef in the world and each one's specialty. He traveled from Paris to Cannes for *moules au vin* in a certain little-known restaurant, and from London to Marseilles for bouillabaisse. He could make an anchorite's mouth water with talk about food.

No matter how amusing the Potash and Perlmutter stories were to his readers, they were only a fraction as amusing as when Monty told them. His stories lost much of their charm when put down on paper. The living words were like songs; the written ones like wings pinned down on that sheet of paper. To his friends he told the same story in a half-dozen different versions before he settled for the one he finally wrote. He would keep Martin, the Algonquin valet, in his room for hours, to

Figure 34. Montague Glass, 1918. *Source*: Public domain.

hear him laugh at one of his stories. Monty is a good listener, as many another storyteller will tell you, on one condition: that you listen to one of his own stories. He tells them by the hour.

Writing a story with a hotel kitchen as a background, Glass asked permission to visit the kitchen of the hotel. Case thought it would be one of those cursory visits of a few minutes, just to convince himself that there actually was a stove and a chef with a white peaked cap to preside over it. But that was not what happened. Monty had a long conversation with the chef and discovered he had lived in a certain region of France which Monty was particularly fond of, chiefly because of its culinary qualities. Having talked regional foods, salads, dressings, and sauces for a while, he discovered that the chef was something of a musician, too, so they discussed operatic arias, and soon Monty gave an imitation of Caruso in *La Juive*, and the chef sang an aria from *Aida*. That over with, they continued to talk about cooking, about great chefs, about the history of certain dishes, and Monty had some suggestions to offer about sauces and dressings. The chef disagreed: "No apple vinegar. It is barbaric. Only wine vinegar." Monty disagreed, but didn't insist.

From dressings, the talk veered to wines and the appropriate wine with the different dishes, a subject in dispute for centuries among real gourmets. The chef disagreed with Monsieur Glass about Chambertin and Pommard: "Pouilly, Monsieur. Pouilly or Vouvray. Nothing else." It was not long before all cooking operations stopped, and the cooks, assistant cooks, and the man in charge of the wine cellar gathered about the storyteller and the chef, to listen to them, open-mouthed. With Monty, one story dragged another one out of his treasure, and that one reminded him of another one, and since he was talking to cooks, most of the stories were about the great chefs, past and present: Escoffier, Brillat-Savarin. It was only when the orders from the dining rooms began to pour in that the cooks woke up to the fact that they had lost two hours, and their menu had to be improvised. Monty withdrew to his suite, happy to have been able to make them forget their duties . . . the very function of a storyteller: to make people forget: "After all, the woman who told the thousand and one night stories made the king forget to order her head cut off."

Everything and everybody was late when Monty was around. On the way down from his room he stopped to tell a story to the elevator man, retarding the elevator. He told stories to the desk clerk, to the man behind the cigar counter, to the bartender, to the bellboys, to the waiters and to the captains: and to each one, a story about his own profession. He wouldn't tell a story about a bellboy to a waiter, or about a desk man to the bartender. He would buttonhole anybody on his way out, just for a moment, to tell them something. He wasn't a storyteller; he was a story fountain. He kept his choice story of the day for Miss Bush, the charming lady in charge of the switchboard. He'd call her from his suite, from a party, from Hollywood, and even from Paris, to tell her a good story.

Monty never lunched or dined alone. He always had at least a half-dozen friends about him, male and female. He was not concerned with their intellect or station in life, but about their discernment of good food. If one mentioned a town in Italy, he would answer with the address of the best hotel and restaurant there. The map of Europe represented to him nothing but eating places. He had traveled from Paris to Bucharest for no other reason than to eat some pastry at the Capsha, a restaurant whose famous pastry outranked its other specialties: "At Capsha's I forgot an appointment with Queen Marie. She forgave me when I told her the truth. She had Capsha pastry brought to her room every day."

It was for Monty that Case devoted a chapter in his book on the brewing of coffee. Few people know that Monty had written a textbook of harmony for young piano students. He gave it to Case as a present. Frank lost the manuscript.

When annoyed, Monty had a witty, biting tongue. To a gushing lady who asked whether he was one of the Virginia Glasses, he replied: "No, Madam. I was born in Manchester and I belong to the cut-glasses."

On another occasion, somebody referred to a man who had just left the table as a "kike." "I've finally discovered the meaning of the word 'kike,'" said Monty. "A kike is a Jew who has just left the room."

~

Until the advent of the movies, stage-door Johnnies were young men who stood at stage doors of theatres to catch a glimpse of their favorite actress. There are many stories about the great enthusiasm aroused by actresses in former days. Admirers would unharness the horses and pull the carriage triumphantly through the streets to her destination. Sarah Bernhardt's admirers started that vogue in Paris. Not to be outdone, Mademoiselle Rachel, the French tragedienne, had herself pulled by students harnessed to her carriage. London, Berlin, Rome, and later, New York, saw similar spectacles. At the turn of the century, the hitching posts in front of the Algonquin saw many a horseless carriage brought to it by noisy manpower. Some of the enthusiasm was genuine; some of it was publicity.

Stage-door Johnnies have now been replaced by fans, a new species of admirers. Young boys and girls crowd about the entrances of theatres and hover about hotels and restaurants, not to catch a glimpse of their favorite, but to get their signatures. There is a sort of stock exchange quoting the value of each signature, a value which is probably a better indication of the popularity of a star than even Mr. Elmo Roper could contrive. The quotations fluctuate. One day it is one Hedy Lamarr for two Loretta Youngs and the next day the opposite is quoted. You can always see the autograph seekers outside of 21, the Colony, the Stork Club, and every restaurant where motion picture and theatrical people congregate. They literally mob those whose signatures are in demand. A signature, once obtained, is often immediately offered for trade for other signatures.

Motion-picture actor Melvyn Douglas, a mutual actress friend, and I were having dinner one night when two ladies, who sat facing Melvyn, became very agitated. They asked the captain's advice as to how to obtain

Mr. Douglas's signature. Finally, one of the women stood up determinedly, but lost her nerve at the last minute, passed the table and left the room. When she finally returned, having steeled herself, she approached Douglas and made her request, gushing that he was the "greatest actor on the screen. It's such a thrill to meet you." The actress's face twitched. She had been off the screen for a year, and the woman was facing her as she pressed Douglas for an autograph, but didn't recognize her. Melvyn obligingly gave the woman his autograph, then left the room. A few minutes later, a dozen people came up to our table, clamoring for the actress's autograph, as Douglas had instructed them.

~

There is not one motion-picture actor who has enjoyed the popularity once held by Rudolph Valentino. Even in star-surfeited Hollywood, he could not show his face without being mobbed by women. While he and I were having Sunday dinner in his famous Eagle's Nest, sight-seeing bus followed sight-seeing bus up the steep hill, and we could hear the motors stop in front of the gate to give the guide an opportunity to shout: "Here lives the great Valentino! That upper window is the window of his bedroom." Sighs. Oohs. Ahs. "Down below is the famous oak-paneled dining room."

Other guides, more imaginative, declaimed about the women who had committed suicide on his doorstep. It was music to the ears of Valentino. He stopped eating, stopped talking, when his name was shouted outside. Though it was a cool day and he was subject to colds, all the windows were open so that the sound of voices should penetrate the whole house.

Publicity was no doubt responsible for the phenomenal attraction of the man, but no publicity about any other actor has ever produced such a mass psychosis. The police had to be called in Chicago to clear a path for him from the hotel lobby to the car outside. When the train on which he was traveling to New York stopped at Needles, California, the crowd invaded the train, broke into his compartment, and shredded his clothes to carry away mementoes. Valentino, of course, pretended not to like the effect he had created, pretended he wanted privacy, but if the craze abated for a day or two, he called in his publicity men and asked what had happened: why there were not as many sight-seeing buses passing his door; why he was not being mobbed; and threatened to fire them. "You are not on the job!" The late June Mathis, his friend,

Figure 35. Rudolph Valentino, c. 1920s. *Source*: Bain News Service, Library of Congress, Prints and Photographs Division.

his mentor, his writer, agent, and factotum, brooked no excuses from the publicity department of the film company.

When Valentino arrived in New York, Grand Central Station was so crowded, people missed outgoing trains. When he walked along Fifth Avenue, there were people only on his side of the street, because people had crossed from the other side to trail along, though he was a thousand feet ahead. Women bribed the laundryman for a Valentino sock, a collar, a handkerchief, or a button from one of his shirts.

One day the great Valentino brought a group of his friends to lunch at the Algonquin. The usual mob had followed to the door. But when he sat down in the Rose Room, none of the other guests showed any surprise. They noticed his entrance and saw him sit down, but there was no to-do about him. His companions, Italians, and at the Algonquin for the first time, looked around, amazed that there was no stir created by the appearance of the idol. The waiters served him with no more deference than they showed other guests, and Georges, the headwaiter, stood at his usual place. Nobody fought for the privilege of entering the dining room.

From where I sat, I could see Valentino's face change color. He was not a particularly handsome man: he had a rather sallow complexion, and his black, patent-leather hair was beginning to thin. He looked like a gigolo, the kind one sees on the Riviera, a dancer waiting for some middle-aged woman to invite him to dance with her, at so much per. He was not a good actor. He wasn't an actor. He was a smooth adagio dancer, but there were many better dancers: better and handsomer and more masculine. He looked like a female impersonator. His love for colored silks, perfume and perfumed cigarettes, and his mincing gait and high voice made his masculinity suspect.

All the publicity in the world could not have created such a psychosis in women. There undoubtedly was something else, which no male can fathom. And he was not intelligent. All the talk about his intellectuality and culture was just so much hogwash. He didn't even speak Italian, his own language, well. Those old enough to remember the newspaper sensation caused by his death have reason to believe that a declaration of war would not have caused a greater sensation, more consternation, in a major element of our population.

And there Valentino sat that morning, with a hundred or more people at adjoining tables, and nobody seemed to take any particular notice of him. After a while he caught my eye and came to my table to shake hands, hoping this would attract attention, but it didn't. Turning to face the room, he asked in a loud and angry whisper: "What's the matter with the people here? Are they all dead? I visited the Institute for the Blind, and even the blind knew when I was there."

"No," I said. "They are not dead. They are hungry."

"But I'm not," Valentino retorted, and he stalked out without retrieving his coat from the cloak room, followed by his muttering companions. There was a mob outside. He stood at the door, breathed deeply, then reached into his pocket, threw at them all the money he had, then grabbed more from his friends and threw that to them, too.

That was the last time Valentino was seen at the Algonquin. Several days later I met him in the studio of a sculptor who was making his bust. He was still bitter about the attitude of the people at the Algonquin: "They are just ignorant peasants. They don't even know how to behave when a sensational artist comes in."

It was useless to tell him that the Algonquin was so inured to sensational people, only the sudden appearance of the Lord would create a "sensation." Mrs. Roosevelt, Hedy Lamarr, Greta Garbo, Paulette Goddard, Gertrude Stein, Rebecca West, Edna St. Vincent Millay, and many other sensational people, to mention only a few of the ladies, have gone up and down the elevators without more than a nod, passed through the lobby, and gone to their tables without attracting more attention than they do in their own homes.

Ours is a scientific age. We accept only the explicable, the tangible, and what can be verified. New scientific discoveries enlarge the horizon of our understanding daily and explain what was a mysterious phenomenon only yesterday. There is no explanation for the aura that hovers about certain personalities and makes them more outstanding even than their work, their achievement, warrants. Any half-observant person has come across individuals who have that certain quality. It is often noticeable in children at an early stage. Some of this aura persists long after the personality has passed on from the living, persists in the minds and the memory of the living, many of whom have had no personal contact with that person.

Rudolph Valentino was far from being a great actor. On his acting ability alone, he couldn't have gotten very far. As an individual, as a man, he wasn't handsome, he wasn't strong, he wasn't masculine, and there was apparently no good reason why so many women, young and old, should have swooned when his shadow appeared on the silver screen. The camera flattered him and made him appear handsomer, stronger, taller than he really was, but that isn't a plausible explanation of the effect he had on his audience. He wasn't a camera-made personality. When he appeared anywhere in person, the adulation was just as spontaneous as when his shadow was thrown on the screen. His death, though at the decline of his career, caused such consternation, the newspapers, realizing the pulse of their readers, pushed everything off the front pages to make place for an obituary few kings have equaled.

The day Valentino died, Queen Marie of Romania arrived in New York, after intensive and clever publicity directed by experts who spared no expense to have her appear a paragon of patriotism and heroism. According to that publicity, she had won World War I by herself and had, by her courageous actions, saved many American soldiers. This is not the place to discuss the truth of such assertions. However, she arrived in New York a well-advertised and important personality, and great preparations had been made for her reception. Romania had been our ally in the war;

the Romanian government had an embassy in Washington and many consular offices in the principal cities of the United States. All official personnel were harnessed to the job of publicity. What passes for society was stimulated to arrange receptions and balls in her honor. Affairs were scheduled at the Metropolitan Opera, for which tickets had been sold at fabulous prices, for the benefit of the Queen's charities. All of that was pushed aside because Rudolph Valentino had died: all of that and many another item that would have been on the front page was relegated to back pages, because Marie arrived on the day of an actor's death.

For years after his death, wreaths placed by mysterious hands appeared on his grave on every anniversary of his demise, and veiled women were seen kneeling and kissing the ground about his tombstone. And for years and years, half a dozen middle-aged ladies reserved the table at which Valentino had once lunched at the Algonquin and, dressed in deep mourning, sat about that table, leaving one chair vacant, and ate, but said not a word to each other. And always, the unused silver on the table before the vacant seat disappeared when they left. The waiter who had served that table when Valentino had come for lunch, did a thriving business out of the superstitions of those women. He sold the forks, spoons, and knives he assured them Valentino had used. He did that year after year, and since the same ladies appeared for that yearly ritual, they should have known that their idol could not possibly have used all the silver they bought. They should have known, but didn't want to know.

Now Valentino had never appeared in a motion picture dealing with the supernatural. There was no hint in any of his pictures of the occult. There was no hint in any of the many stories of his life that he believed in or practiced the occult. He was, of course, caught in the web of the noise made about his personality and was childish enough to wind up believing some of the things thought up by the studio's publicity experts. Generally speaking, he was interested in his box office value to the studio and to himself. "What's the good of being lucky if you don't cash in on your luck?" June Mathis used to say, when she demanded more money from the studio.

What then? What was there about him to have made such an outstanding specimen of him in life as well as in death? Publicity alone couldn't have done it. Other actors of the screen have since had greater publicity, but not one has achieved such popularity, or made such an impression. I don't know the answer, but that doesn't mean there is no answer.

His aura is not yet dead. On a certain day of the year, some elderly ladies in black still lunch at that table and keep a chair vacant, telling the waiter that they expect a friend for lunch; a friend who never comes, but whom they pretend to see.

～

The last century has seen many prominent magicians and sleight-of-hand artists. Seen from the stage, some of their manipulations defy any reasonable explanation. The rabbits pulled out of the hat, the disappearance and reappearance of gilded cages alive with twittering canaries, the women sawed in half, and the breaking of all shackles are witnessed, not as supernatural miracles, but as mechanical contrivances that create illusions. Even children know that what they see are tricks, and nothing but tricks.

The late Harry Houdini was, no doubt, one of the cleverest performers. When he did his daily stint at the Hippodrome, just across the street from the Algonquin, he lived at the hotel. His suite was crammed with trunks and boxes that contained the paraphernalia of his acts. A special engineer was occupied daily in the suite to keep the instruments in condition and to invent new ones. Houdini himself was a very ingenious mechanic, who did not rely on old acts to keep his reputation. When some other magician copied one of his tricks, Houdini abandoned it and created something new.

Houdini looked like a prosperous salesman, and talked like one, but there was that inexplicable aura about him which carried on after his death. His death made a deep impression on the people who knew him, who came in contact with him, who assisted him in his stage tricks. To assure himself of posterity in the minds of the people, he left a will saying that if an afterlife existed, his spirit would return to earth at a certain date and that he would communicate to certain people a report on the world beyond. Whether or not one believes that Houdini believed in the supernatural—he, who by clever mechanical devices created the illusion of the supernatural—is of no importance. The fact is that many believed and waited, and some are still waiting, to hear from him; lawyers and hard-headed businessmen, bankers, ministers, and artists. Even some professional magicians believe that Houdini's performances were not all mechanical; that he did have some occult power. Because they cannot duplicate his tricks, they assert that they were not tricks at all,

Figure 36. Harry Houdini, c. 1913. *Source*: Library of Congress, Prints and Photographs Division.

but supernatural manifestations. It is quite possible that Houdini himself didn't believe that all he did was merely due to his own cleverness.

Because they were befriended by him, some people are waiting for his spirit to reappear, to communicate with them. While waiting, they spread their beliefs to others. Hotel attendants, who had seen the tremendous array of paraphernalia he used, who had seen him tinker and work to perfect shackles and other instruments, believe, or pretend to believe, in Houdini's supernatural powers. And they, too, are waiting. People one seldom sees the whole year 'round come casually and sit in the lobby, or lunch in the dining room and look abstractedly at the ceiling on certain days. Some reserve his suite for a particular day, pull down the shades, and wait.

I imagine that similar things happen in every old hotel. Bereaved people who have read the romantics, the stories in which there is a secret room in every castle, are easily convinced that the spirit doesn't die with the body. And even when they don't believe in it exactly, it does their soul good to commune with themselves on a certain day in the room once occupied by their beloved. Considering that many of the people who live at the Algonquin have had wide circles of admirers, it is little wonder that there are many more such anniversaries than in other hotels.

There was an aura about the poetess, Elinor Wylie. Tall, slender, ethereal, she looked like an apparition. I am not prepared to say that she was the greatest poet or prose writer, yet a certain nimbus hovered about her and her work which cannot be explained on the grounds of cleverness, ability, or talent. People who didn't know who she was kept at a distance from her, though there was no aloofness in her behavior. She was, as a matter of fact, the friendliest of people, ready to greet people she didn't know with a smile. Curiously enough, women who have, in general, no appreciation of their own sex and always look with suspicion on the achievements of one of them, held Elinor Wylie in great admiration. Even those intimates who didn't approve of her life never verbally expressed themselves otherwise than with respect when they spoke of her. Whatever Elinor Wylie did was above criticism. They always spoke of her as Elinor Wylie, using both names.

Having passed her table at lunch, without greeting her because she looked as if her mind was elsewhere, she called me back and asked: "What have I done to you not to be recognized?" I assured her that she was wrong; that I hadn't wanted to disturb her. After a few moments, she began to spin a story about someone we both knew. She kept mentioning the name of the person, but the facts were inventions and had little relation to the character of that person. The woman she spoke about was then in England, and happily married, and not in California having an affair with an Indian. Her food and coffee were untouched and she kept on talking, not to me: to herself. I left the table on tiptoe, not to disturb her, and watched her from another table, as she continued to tell herself the story.

She, too, left an indelible impression upon people, more so by something in the makeup of her personality than by her actual work, beautiful as it is. I remember the expression she used about another writer whom she loved and respected: "She has no shamanism! There is no magic about her. It is all too conscious. Not contrived, but conscious. She works at it." Elinor Wylie was a shaman; a witch doctor. God knows how Elinor herself slaved over a poem or a story, writing and rewriting everything a dozen times. But the finished product read like an inspiration. Knowing my interest in Gypsies, she added, speaking about that woman poet: "What she does and what someone else we both know does, is the difference between a musician's composition and the improvisation of a Gypsy." I took her down to the East Side of New York, to a Gypsy restaurant. She became so absorbed in the music, she didn't say a word the whole evening, nor did she eat or drink. She just listened. She was still listening when they stopped playing hours after midnight, when I took her home.

Shortly after her death, the desk clerk of the hotel told me that several women had come, one after the other, and asked to see the room Elinor Wylie had occupied when she stayed at the hotel. What did they expect to see or find there? Hundreds of other people have since occupied that room. Few people were as conscious of the "shaman" quality in an artist as Elinor Wylie was.

I don't believe in the supernatural. I don't believe in the occult; not in the vulgar term of the word. I believe there is a plausible explanation for everything. The fact that we have no explanation for a phenomena does not deny the existence of the phenomena; and so, for want of any other word, I call aura the unseen nimbus that hovers about certain persons, and persists in the memories of other people long after their death. I believe that people see ghosts only because they believe in ghosts. I believe such a belief is a vulgarization of the belief in the immortality of the soul. The human mind is an ethereal wax and can be molded into every possible form.

Man is the kind of dreams he has, the kind of desires he has, the hopes and loves he has. Man is shaped from within.

~

Edward O'Brien, the man who for more than twenty years published the yearly book of the best American short stories, a Canadian who lived in England, would come every year to New York for the final touches to the collection of what he considered the best short stories published that year. When I remarked that he frequently published "best" stories that were far from being the best, he replied that he, too, knew it; yet he came every year, not only for the final arrangements of the publication of the book, but to meet the people whose stories he printed. He had often come to New York with stories he had decided upon as best, and abandoned publication after meeting the author. "There didn't seem to be any relation between the person and what they have done," he explained. "On the other hand, there are stories that neither you nor I would consider the best, but there is something about the person who wrote them that makes me feel that they and what they did is one; that the story is not only of the mind and of the hand."

Whenever he was in New York, his room at the Algonquin was filled twenty-four hours a day. Some people are insatiable drinkers, others are chain-smokers. O'Brien's weakness was an insatiable curiosity. All kinds of people, young, old, men, women, artists, artisans, writers, musicians, street cleaners, came to see him.

Why O'Brien, who had great gifts as a writer, should have considered the collection of short stories his life work is a mystery. The money he got could not have been the only motive. The poetic biography he wrote of Friedrich Nietzsche comes nearer an explanation of the man. He considered Nietzsche the greatest of all philosophers and poets, the apostle of greatness, the enemy of mediocrity.

O'Brien told the most fantastic stories. His tales were all tall, yet I can name twenty people who heard him one day predict, almost to the day, the death of his friend, T. E. Lawrence, known as Lawrence of Arabia, whom he had left well and hearty only a week before. Lawrence was an extraordinary figure. As a British agent, he had made himself the uncrowned King of Arabia and, by organizing the Arabs, a feat never duplicated before or since, he had defeated the Turkish armies and laid the foundations of several Arab countries. In the end, he disagreed profoundly with the British government on Arab policy and became a stormy petrel. As a descriptive writer, he has no equal in the English language. "There will be all kinds of explanations. But I am the only one to know what is going to happen," O'Brien assured us.

"Eddie, you're laying yourself wide open," someone said. "You're sticking your neck out. You've told other tall tales."

"I know he is soon going to die a violent death."

"But why be so precise about the date? I'll bet you a hundred dollars to one that it won't happen within three months of the date." Joe Anthony, author of *The Gang*, *The Golden Village*, and other books that will eventually become classics in America, accepted the bet instead of O'Brien, and won. Lawrence had a fatal motorcycle accident that has never been explained.

The O'Brien collection was eagerly awaited every year; the publication of the best short stories since his death passes almost unobserved. Yet whenever there is talk about O'Brien, there is hardly any mention of his work, not even of the yearly book, but only of the man.

~

Panaite, the Macedonian waiter who had waited on Valentino, used to work in another restaurant on his weekly day off. He was an intellectual. Georges, the headwaiter, a graduate of the University of Athens, held Panaite in great esteem. Though he had no degree from any college, the man had picked up a ponderous quantity of intellectual baggage, spoke English, French, and Spanish beautifully, and there wasn't a subject of which he didn't have the latest slant. When not too busy, he leaned against a customer's table and delivered his opinions on politics, the latest play, the latest book, and wasn't shy about expressing his opinions of the customer's latest, whatever it was.

Panaite was a likeable fellow, but Freud ruined him. He began to see complexes in everything; in the meal you ordered, in the manner in which it was ordered, and would suddenly remark: "That's three days in succession you have ordered veal. Why?" Or: "Your ties are louder than they used to be. Why?" Or: "He comes here with his mother twice a week. When he is with his mother, he never looks at another woman." "Pablo Casals, the great cellist, had lunch here yesterday. Have you ever noticed his mincing gait? All cellists have mincing gaits." Panaite loved and understood great music. He owned a tremendous library of phonograph records. All his life he had enjoyed listening to music: after reading Freud he began to criticize music from the Freudian angle.

Because his own outlook had been warped by the reading of Freud, he began to see a warped personality in everybody. The writers, musicians, and actors he had admired became so many "sublimators," and he attempted to find out, by the Socratic method, what each one was sublimating. After a while, the guests got tired of answering his questions. Eventually, the Algonquin appeared to him like an insane asylum. What had been idiosyncrasies in a guest was interpreted as a form of insanity, proving once again how dangerous a little learning can be. Once a week, on his free day, Panaite was a waiter in another restaurant; not for the extra money, but to restore his sanity "by being once a week with average, normal people." Eventually the "normal" people ceased to appear normal to him, and he took a job in another restaurant. To the question why he didn't reverse the process, work six days a week in a restaurant catering to "normal" people and only once a week in an exceptional and abnormal atmosphere, Panaite replied that he had become conditioned to abnormality. More Freud.

Panaite admired Franklin P. Adams, and detested Alexander Woollcott. He maintained that Woollcott had been a big, fat, caponized cat in a previous existence. His study of the Freudian theory had not weaned Panaite from a belief in the transmigration of souls. The last I heard of Panaite, he was living in Athens, where he has written a book of studies about the abnormalities of American writers and artists; a book in which I occupy a number of pages. He seems to have read everything every one of the guests he once served wrote, and bases his observations, clinical, of course, on the recurrence of certain words in each one's stories and novels. Food preferences of the respective writers are also analyzed in detail.

~

When I was employed on the *New York World*, at a time when Heywood Broun, F. P. A., Alexander Woollcott, Deems Taylor, and Laurence Stallings graced one of the pages of that paper, an artist in the Sunday edition department was assigned to illustrate my weekly stories. Though the paper paid high salaries to its stars, it wasn't too generous to writers and artists ranking second or third from the top.

Louis, my illustrator, fat and Teutonic, was, among other things, the banker of the Sunday department. We were paid on Friday, but most of the people ran out of cash by Monday or Tuesday, and Louis was always willing to advance five or ten dollars to his colleagues until payday. The way to approach him was to offer him a cigar, whereupon he would ask: "How much do you want? And don't ask for too much. I already have four cigars in my pocket." On payday, each of his debtors gave Louis another cigar: a five-cent one for a five-dollar loan, a ten-cent one for a ten-dollar loan.

Louis and I worked at adjoining desks and enjoyed many discussions about the old country. He had lived in the United States for forty years, but was as German as when he had first set foot on American soil; if not more so. When he discovered that I had lived in Wiesbaden a few years, he was overjoyed. Wiesbaden was his home town. Louis was a peculiar man and very tight about money, but he was a well-educated person with ideas and ideals.

At one time, needing a loan, a rather larger one than Louis usually made, I asked Louis for the money and proposed to pay the sum off in three weekly installments. Louis refused point-blank. "All the other people here are very simple people," he explained. "People without ideas. Lend them ten dollars and at the end of the week they'll repay you. But you are a man of ideas. How do I know what ideas you'll have at the end of the week, or the second or third week? An idea to leave the place maybe? An idea not to pay me? To men of ideas I lend no money to be paid back in three weeks."

His contract with the paper stipulated that Louis was not to do any work for any other daily or weekly paper. But one day it was discovered that he was drawing cartoons for a rival paper. His work was so individual it was easily recognized, even without his signature. Called on the carpet by the manager, who asked whether he didn't know what his contract specified, Louis replied: "I do."

"Then why did you draw for another paper?"

Louis, who had no ideas, answered: "To earn enough money to enable me to keep my job on the *New York World*."

When asked why he worked for the *World* for what he considered insufficient pay, he shouted, pointing to each of the men in the room: "Because of him, because of him, because of you. Because there is something about this damn place that makes me want to stay here; that makes all of us want to stay here for such miserable pay. This isn't a job. It's a vice, like dope."

There was something about the *New York World* yet to be explained. No demise of any paper caused such mourning all over the country. Books have been written about the "end of the *World*."

All the employees stood vigil the night before the *World* passed out of existence. This attitude wasn't all due to the quality of the paper, and not to the columnists who made the paper and themselves famous. That last vigil of the *New York World* is repeated every time two or more of the former employees meet. I've talked to linotypers and press men, who had nothing to do with the editorial quality of the paper, but they, too, though now working on other papers, have a nostalgic feeling for the *World*.

We, of the twelfth floor, where the Sunday magazine section was edited, had our own round table at Garbarino's saloon, on Pearl Street. It is now over twenty years since the *New York World* disappeared, but I have never yet been at Garbarino's without finding some of my former coworkers sitting at our old table, with a glass of beer before them, talking about "them were the days": former coworkers who are now famous editors, writers, and illustrators.

There is nothing about Joe Garbarino's saloon one could call atmospheric. It's just an ordinary saloon frequented by printers and mechanics working in the neighborhood. Occasionally, one or another of my former coworkers comes to the Algonquin, for no other reason but to chew the rag, to retaste the flavor of the past, to recriminate about the poor pay and bad working conditions they once had on the *New York World*. A man who had a high position in the administration of the *World* was given a similar position by the paper's successor. But he couldn't hold the new job, and eventually, after going through several jobs on other papers, became a chicken farmer. "I just couldn't work on another paper. No atmosphere." He looked at me steadily. "Do you get it? No atmosphere."

"I get it."

"My wife and daughters don't get it at all. That's why I come to see you. You get it."

~

The Bodnes, now referred to as "The Algonquin Bodnes," are a clan. To see them together, father, mother and the two daughters, Renee Mae and Barbara, one realizes that the ties that bind them are not the ordinary parental and filial chorus; they treat each other and talk to each other as if they were all of the same age. Ben B. Bodne had to begin to earn his bread before the age of eleven, and was a millionaire at forty. No one has acquired a fortune at that age without a dominant instinct of possession, and Ben is no exception. How it was possible to follow that instinct without acquiring also a domineering attitude towards one's family, I don't know.

The Bodnes are a clan: but a clan of four individualists, endowed by nature or conditioned to tolerate each other's differences. The girls, the older of whom is not yet twenty, don't look alike and don't dress alike and have different inclinations.

Ben B. Bodne leans far back in his chair on a sunny day, and says in his Southern drawl: "I am going to get a car and ride me to the baseball game this afternoon."

To which Mrs. Bodne rejoins: "You only say so. You'll go upstairs and watch the game on the television set."

"I could do that and be more comfortable," he assents, "but since you put it that way, I propose that we both go to the ball game. We'll get some sunshine and maybe a little excitement, too."

"No. You go. I'm going shopping with the girls."

"Shopping?"

"Yes, shopping. It's more fun than watching a ball being thrown."

Barbara, the youngest, approaches. "You all going shopping with your mother, Barbara?"

"Me? No. I am going to the library to read up on something. There is nothing in the shops I want."

Renee Mae comes up shortly. "Going shopping with your mother this afternoon, Renee Mae"?"

"No. Don't think so. I was figuring on going to a matinee."

"To see what?"

"*South Pacific.*"

"You saw it twice."

"Could see it again."

"I'm going upstairs to watch the ball game on the television set."

Ben is a baseball fan. He has played the game and at one time had hoped to become a professional. He can talk baseball by the hour and reminds his listeners: "I once wanted to buy me a baseball company. Yes sir, wanted to buy me a baseball outfit all my own."

The Bodnes have a car and chauffeur in front of the hotel. Any one of the family uses the "outfit" when it is free, without inquiring, or permission.

Despite the fact that Mr. Bodne has spent $50,000 on new kitchen installations to bring it up to the most modern standard, and has hired the best chef to preside over it, the Bodnes eat out very often. "We always did eat out a good deal. Sometimes when there was the best dinner ready to be served, one of us would say 'let's eat out tonight' and out we ate, and then went to the theatre. I'd be troubled about business, a deal that didn't jell, machinery that broke down, labor troubles, all that sort of thing, and I'd come home and tell Mrs. Bodne: 'Let's eat out and see a show tonight.' She never said no. By the time the show was half over, I had forgotten my troubles. And if you can forget about troubles, you don't have them."

All the Bodnes love the theatre. Without being stage-struck, the girls, as well as their parents, know everything and everybody in the theatre. To them, the chief value of owning the Algonquin is in being close to what's going on in the theatre and in the fact that there are so many theatrical folk living there. They celebrate anniversaries by going to the theatre. When they meet someone they like, they invite them to a theatre party. They see the plays they like over and over again, but not always together. On certain nights, the four Bodnes see four different plays.

At lunch time, it is no rarity to see Ben and his friends lunching at one table, Mrs. Bodne and friends at another table, and their two daughters lunching separately with their friends and only getting together for coffee in the lobby or upstairs in their apartment, or in Renee Mae's apartment, which was redecorated to suit the taste of her young husband, in the process of being absorbed into his wife's family.

At one time, during the deal for the Algonquin, Mr. Bodne let it be known that he was going to buy another hotel instead. Promptly the two daughters informed their parents that if another hotel was bought, they would return to Charleston: they wouldn't live in New York if they didn't live at the Algonquin. They weren't interested just in hotels. For years they had heard their parents mention the Algonquin. Now it was going to be it or nothing.

When Bodne became the president of the Tournament of Champions, sportswriters wrote that he had become the head of the T. C. to assure himself of two good tickets for each of the proposed fights. When he bought the Algonquin, columnists jibed that he had bought the hotel because he wanted a room under its roof. I don't know about the motives behind the organization of the Tournament of Champions, but there is more than a grain of truth in what the columnists said about the purchase of the hotel. He said, "I closed the deal sooner than I should have, because I didn't want to break up the family. If I had bought another hotel and Barbara would have refused to stay in New York, I wouldn't have compelled her. So, she and her mother would have lived in Charleston, and it would have been hard on all of us, a mess of traveling back and forth."

"Isn't that indulging your daughter a little too much?"

"No, I don't think so. I wish I had five more like her and her sister. The deal turned out OK; I knew it would. Of course, I had lawyers and accountants go over everything. After all, you don't invest more than a million dollars on someone's say-so. But I have an instinct for such things. When I feel like doing something, I know it will turn out well. When I don't want to go into a deal, lawyers and accountants may show me it's the best deal in the world; if I have a premonition, if my instinct says no, it's no. That's how it's been all my life. I have always lost money when I didn't follow my instinct. People say I am psychic that way. Whatever that is, it's so.

"You have no idea how many people warned me against buying the Algonquin. 'Ben, you are buying a headache. Ben, you'll lose your shirt. Ben, labor troubles will wear you down.' Every one said something else. 'Why don't you stay in Charleston. It's been good to you.' It certainly has been good to me. And I love Charleston. But we have never been happier than we are now. This hotel is the kind of place that suits us; we meet the kind of people we like."

One day, an employee's irregularities having been discovered, Bodne discussed the matter with his family. The first thing they wanted established was that the person in question wouldn't be legally prosecuted. The next question was whether he should be dismissed or kept on, with a severe reprimand. Bodne insisted that the employee be dismissed: he could not be kept on. That settled, Mr. Bodne talked the matter over with his manager. The culprit was so disliked by the manager and his assistant, they flipped a coin as to who should fire him. The manager won.

But until the man was out of the building, none of the Bodnes came down from their apartments. They were embarrassed for the man's sake. Should their common antagonism be aroused, they'd be like a wall, through which no appeal to sympathy could penetrate. A slighting remark made about one of their intimates by a pivotal man in the organization was enough to have him out on his ears before the day was over. "Pay him off and get him out," the Bodnes clamored.

Ben B. Bodne hasn't given up his oil and other interests in the South. He often has to be away from home for short periods of time. When that happens, the wires are kept busy between him and his family. He has to tell them everything—whom he has seen, what he has eaten, how he is. And they have to tell him everything about themselves and the hotel, including who, of note, has arrived and where they have been put up.

"Couldn't you have put him in 1205? I think he would have liked he color of the walls better."

"1205 is not free."

"Anybody I know there?"

"Mr. and Mrs. R ——."

"Send them up some flowers."

"It's been done."

What was to be a side investment, a sentimental investment, has by now become his principal concern. The redecoration of the few hundred rooms, done piecemeal, so as not to make people aware that a general renovation is taking place, has taken three years and was done in so unobtrusive a manner, few people noticed the change. Only guests who had been absent a long time noticed, when they entered their suite, that it had been repainted, that the carpets had been replaced, that the bathroom had been modernized, and noticed the general changes in the hallways and the lobby. Because Mr. Mitchell is at the same desk he has been at for forty years, Miss Bush at the phone, John in the Rose Room, and Raul in the Oak Room, and because Nick, the oldest employee in the hotel, with nearly forty years of service, is still serving breakfast in the rooms, and Martin, the valet, comes to take your clothes to be cleaned, one forgets that new owners are running the Algonquin.

A great quality of the Bodnes is their unobtrusiveness. They are here. Their mark is everywhere. Their presence is felt, but not oppressively. They don't attempt to fill anyone's shoes. They walk in their own. A lady from California who met Mr. Bodne for the first time, said: "I am so glad you have made no changes in the hotel after Mr. Case's death. It would have been dreadful if you had."

"It was a great compliment," Bodne remarked. "I've spent a quarter of a million dollars and three years to renovate the place, and it was so well done she didn't notice it."

"Do you mean it? Do you mean you are glad she didn't notice it?"

"Mean it? I sent flowers up to her room. Of course I mean it. I did better than Mr. Case, when he redecorated Hitchcock's room, didn't I? And after all, Mr. Case had had years of experience with his clientele by then. But this is really a compliment for Mary, Mrs. Bodne. She is in charge of these things. She's an extraordinary woman. She puts on the most expensive new dress and it will not look as if she has put it on to show off, and she can wear an old dress and you'd swear it's just out of the box. The girls, too, are like that. I put on a new suit and feel as if everybody notices it: everybody is saying, 'Look at Ben. He has a new suit on.'

"Yes sir, I sent flowers up to the lady and got her a pair of tickets to the most popular show in town. What I like people to really notice is what I have done to the kitchen. But nobody goes there. I have to drag people to show them what I have done. I left one corner just as it was when I took over, so people could see the difference. What a difference!"

Ben Bodne's eyes sparkle when he tells of the birth of his interest in the theatre. There was an old theatre in Charleston that was to be torn down to make room for a new one. It was such a solidly built edifice, with such thick stone walls, professional wreckers wouldn't have any part of the business for the price offered. Ben, a young man then, went over to have a look. Though he didn't know more about the wrecking business than he knew of the hotel business twenty years later, he thought it could be done profitably. The professionals warned him. They more they warned him, the more his interest was aroused. He went back to look at the old theatre again and again. Knowing something of the value of old building materials, he began to figure the cost of tearing the thing down, as against the sales value of the salvaged material: the iron, the lead, the extra heavy and long beams. He talked the matter over again with the professionals, quoting figures to them. They quoted different figures, higher costs for the wrecking operations, and lower values for the salvaged material. People were always crippled or killed in such operations; accidents that involved costly lawsuits, no matter how one protected himself with insurance companies. There was always the factor of negligence, of lack of ordinary precaution.

Ben watched the professionals on another job and concluded that they were using old-fashioned methods. After carefully canvassing the field, he hired an engineer who laid out a plan as to how the work should be done with a minimum of risk. Bodne contracted for the job, finished it without a major accident, and wound up with a larger bank account than he had had when he started, although he sold some of the material to get immediately needed cash, for much less than it was worth.

When the new theatre was finished on the site of the old one, he attended its dedication and opening night. "And I've been a theatre fan ever since."

But did he continue in the wrecking business? No. "It's too involved and risky. I couldn't sleep nights, thinking of the danger to the people working for me. I worried myself sick. I'm in business to make money. But no amount of money is worth my health. I did it only because they said it couldn't be done for what there was in it. My instincts told me it could be done." Ben seldom says, "I know I'm right." He always says, "I feel I'm right."

"I have learned how to protect myself. Get the best doctor when you are sick. Get the best lawyer to tell you where you are wrong and then go ahead. Harry Hershfield told a good doctor-lawyer story the other day.

"A man who had had three heart attacks—such bad attacks that he was compelled to stay away from his business—won a million dollars in the sweepstakes. The family rejoiced, but were afraid to tell the news to the sick man, fearing the excitement might prove fatal. So they consulted their lawyer to find out if the check could be cashed without the sick man finding out about it all at once. The lawyer said it couldn't be done, but agreed to talk the matter over with the heart specialist who was attending the sick man.

"The next day the doctor visited the patient, and while massaging him softly about the region of the heart, said casually: 'By the way, my friend, I hear you won the million-dollar sweepstakes. Aren't you a lucky guy!'

"'If I have won the million-dollar sweepstakes, I'll give you half of it,' the sick man said.

The doctor dropped dead."

Talking about plunging into new business, Bodne tells the story of how at one time he was the successful bidder to furnish thirty-seven out of forty-two items needed by the War Department. His competitors were certain he would not be able to furnish them, due to their scarcity. It was a challenge. Ben went to Washington, and, on the strength of his successful bids, obtained priority on one item after the other, from the different authorities apportioning the respective materials.

"It was a job," he mused reminiscently. "But in the end, I furnished all the thirty-seven items in the quantities demanded by the War Department, and got the reputation of a man who delivers. I did many other things people said couldn't be done. I've made mistakes, of course, but my right guesses outweighed them. I am a lucky guy.

"I built a deep water pier in Charleston when most everybody said it couldn't be done, and that if it could be done, it wouldn't be profitable. I built it and it was profitable. I became known in Charleston and in New Orleans and all over the South as the man who'd buy anything that was put up for sale and sell anything that was obtainable. I was my own boss and did all my plunging on my own. Ben B. Bodne was and is the Ben B. Bodne Company."

Ben tells these stories of his struggles to wealth, not in a boasting tone, but to prove that an average American, industrious and willing to take a chance, has all the avenues to success open to him: "It's like this hotel. I love it. Mr. Case did a marvelous job in building up its clientele and creating a unique atmosphere. I'd sooner own it than anything else I own or have owned. But it has a lot of quirks that have to be ironed out and taken out. No one sees them. No one has seen them. I didn't see them when I bought the place. But I see them now and remedy them as I go along. A lot of old equipment looked better than it really was. The cellars and the basement are crowded with old motors and old machines, obsolete and broken down. When everybody is asleep, the old stuff is carted out and new things are carried in—new motors, new refrigerators, new air-conditioning machines, new ice machines. It's a job. Atmosphere is wonderful, but you have to give a lot of other things with it to keep people happy."

Mrs. Bodne was talking about styles one day, and remarked how a vogue was created by having distinguished ladies initiate it. By the time the vogue is created, the distinguished ladies have to wear something else to maintain their distinction. Occasionally a new style catches on so well it kills itself; like the Eugenie hat. It flattered every woman, young, old, blonde, brunette, oval-faced, round-faced. Within a few months, twenty million women wore Eugenie hats, and suddenly it was off. It had killed itself by its own popularity.

Barbara Bodne, the youngest, remarked that the same thing happened to certain words. They lend distinction when they are first used, but when they become too popular, the very people who had first used them in stories and novels, drop them. When asked for an example, she said: "Take the word 'complex.' Everything was 'complex' until a year or two ago. Or the word 'divine.' All the girls used it. They don't, anymore."

Bernard Sobel, columnist and biographer of the great Ziegfeld, told how he, Frank Case, and a few others were talking of styles late one night in the lobby, when someone mentioned the great number of stories, novels, and plays that were written on the subject of pearl necklaces, after Maupassant's story, "The Pearl Necklace," had appeared. For years and years, almost every writer, from Zamacois to Somerset Maugham produced at least one necklace story, in Germany, in England, in the Scandinavian countries, Italy, Russia, Hungary, and even in Turkey. The vogue of the necklace sailed over to the United States and forthwith there were several plays on the boards involving pearl necklaces.

Each one of the Sobel-Case group remembered one or more similar stories and Frank was reenacting—with gestures—the scene from a play in which the star threw a valuable necklace out of the window.

Suddenly there was a loud cry from a lady sitting beside a gentleman opposite Sobel and Case. The string of her pearl necklace had broken, and the pearls were strewn all over the carpet. For the next few hours, Frank Case, Sobel, the lady and the others crawled on the floor, on all fours, picking up pearls until the last one was found. That done, they talked till morning about that coincidence and told more stories about other coincidences, when Frank suddenly remembered that he had not finished the scene in the act and went at it da capo: "Villain! Your pearls shall not buy my honor!"

~

Frank Case's relations to the employees of the hotel, from manager to the last bellboy, were paternal. He kept all of them at arm's length, seldom engaged in friendly conversation with them, frowned when he noticed any familiarity between them and the guests; yet he had a family interest in them, in their welfare, and kept himself informed about them. He was also a disciplinarian. When an employee spoke to him, he had to stand erect, at a respectful distance, and not with their hands in their pockets. Straight as a ramrod himself, with the bearing of a soldier, he exacted the same bearing from them. Under such circumstances, and in this age, one would expect a maximum turnover of employees. But the contrary happened.

When a man at the desk, the bar, or a waiter was replaced, half a dozen men in succession would appear and disappear, one holding the job a week, the next one a month, but once a new man survived three months, he became a fixture and functioned smoothly with the others. There are at present in the hotel men and women, in high and low positions of employment, with forty years of service; men and women who know every nook and cranny, who understand each other and fit into each other's service in a perfect meshing, men and women who know almost every client and their whims and idiosyncrasies, and cater to them without the smile that says, "OK. You're crazy, but what can I do?"

You tell your waiter that you don't want any paprika on your Boston scrod and there won't be any until you ask for it. You ask three people for lunch and the three will be served whipped cream on their Jell-O, and yours won't have any. There will never be ice in your water glass if you have once said you don't want it. If you prefer the second table from the right, though you don't come every day, John will reserve that table for you a reasonable time, though fifty other people clamor for a table. And if he finally lets someone else have it, and you appear after your usual hour, he will explain the matter to you. And it doesn't depend on how heavily you tip him. It depends on whether you are part of the whole scheme. There are men and women who have been coming regularly to the Algonquin for twenty years or more, but are not part of it. Others have come irregularly a lesser number of years, but somehow belong to and with the Algonquin.

Ben Bodne says: "One fellow comes and asks, 'Can I have my room?' The next fellow asks, 'Can I have a room?' It's the first one I want, even if his bill is more difficult to fill. The one who wants *his* room is the one who has made this hotel. The clerk looks to see what room he had a month ago, or last year, and if he can give it to him, we are all happy. If he can't, he is instructed to give him the next best, until we can give him his room."

If Mr. Mitchell is on duty when a guest arrives, he knows who it is. The chances are they use Christian names.

"Hello Mel."

"Hello pop."

"Can't give you your room today. Will do so tomorrow. How is the missus?"

Mitchell may not have seen the man in years.

While I was recuperating in a hospital when my own family was in Europe, Frank Case came to see me and said: "I am fixing up your room with a chaise longue. I'll give Miss Bush the numbers of the only phone calls you wish to receive. What's your diet?" When I was ready to leave the hospital, he came for me: "I've come to take you home." If I were to write the epitaph on Frank Case's tombstone, I'd engrave the following words: "Here lies a man who created a home for many."

I know that people will say Case practiced a kindliness and friendliness that paid off well in the long run. To which I would retort: "I'm glad it did. I'm glad it paid off better than would the contrary."

~

An employee who has been at the Algonquin only ten years is a new-comer. There are bell boys who came to work during the school vacation and remained until they turned gray. Other former bellboys are now members of the stock exchange, are big industrialists and bankers. There was a Filipino bellboy who became a pilot during the war and eventually was raised to the rank of colonel and given several medals for heroic service beyond the call of duty. He visited the Algonquin during one of his furloughs, dined with the Cases, and was feted by everyone. The war over, he was very disappointed not to be given back his place. To the argument that he had been a commanding officer and shouldn't step down to his former position, he answered simply: "But I like it here. It's what I was thinking about all the time I was flying: when the war is over, I'll get my job back." He is in commercial aviation now, but appears in the lobby, and occasionally in the dining room, to satisfy his nostalgia.

Those of us who knew Georges, the former headwaiter of the Rose Room, go to see him once in a while at his new job. He is making more money than he did at the Algonquin, but the sight of an old familiar face brings color to his cheeks as he comes forward with outstretched hands and asks about the guests he had once served. He was one of the mourners at van Loon's and Broun's funerals. Another waiter, Paul, now serving at Antoine's in New Orleans, sends out Christmas cards to his writer and actor friends, and if any of them dines at Antoine's, he demands the privilege of serving them just for the joy of being able to exchange a few words with an Algonquinite.

Paul told me an amusing story: A young man, accompanied by a charming young lady, came in one evening to the Algonquin and ordered a splendid dinner, with several rounds of cocktails to precede the breast of guinea hen, wine, champagne, crepes suzettes, and cognac—the whole works. They were a very gay couple; and Paul, a Macedonian with imagination, tried to figure out whether they were celebrating their engagement or their elopement. After coffee, the young man called for the check. Suddenly he became very excited. His wallet was gone. He looked through all the pockets, under the table, and the girl, too, helped him with the search.

"How much did you have in the wallet?" Paul asked.

"Five hundred dollars. We just came to town for a few days," the young lady volunteered.

The dinner check came to close to fifty dollars. The kids had done themselves proud.

"I'll tell you what," the young man said to the waiter. "I'll leave you my watch until the morning, when I'll get the money by wire from my father in Chicago."

Paul looked at the boy, the girl and the watch, and said: "No need for that. I'll pay it for you. You'll give it back to me tomorrow. I am here at noon."

"Did you lose the theatre tickets, too?" the girl asked the young man.

"Everything. It was all in the wallet."

So Paul, having gone that far, asked: "Will twenty dollars do until you hear from home?"

"That would be wonderful," the young man said. But before taking the money, he pulled out a checkbook. "I should have thought of this. I'll give you a check for the whole thing."

With the twenty dollars, the bill amounted to sixty-seven dollars. The fellow wrote out a check for eighty dollars and handed it to Paul. The check bounced back: no account. Paul gave it up as a total loss. Then, one evening, the young people came into the dining room. "Don't shoot," the young man said to Paul, who moved in on them. "It was a bet. I've brought you the money. Cash." And he counted out the money. Then they sat down to dinner. They were psychology students. But they should have been actors.

"I've never seen a better piece of acting than those two kids showed," Paul said. "'Did you have the money on you that time?' I asked.

"'No, we didn't. That was the whole idea. Not to pay for the dinner, to get money out of you on top of it, and give you a no-good check and get away with it!'"

Raul tells the story of a man who came in one morning and sat down at a table without removing his hat and coat. When the waiter approached him, he said gruffly: "Bring me a bowl, a glass of water, and a spoon." When the waiter had brought those things, the man took a package of dry cereal from one pocket and a bottle of milk from the other, poured them into the bowl, and ate his breakfast, still without removing his hat and coat. The meal finished, he walked out. At the door, he turned to Raul and said: "What I did was an experiment in psychology. Tell me: what was your reaction to such uncommon behavior?"

"The truth?" Raul asked. "You want to know the truth? I thought you were crazy. I still think so."

John, the magician-headwaiter, tells how a rather flashily dressed, middle-aged man, who used to come for dinner occasionally, gave him a hundred dollar bill one night, and said: "I'll be here one of these evenings with a lady: a classy dame. I want you to serve us the best and most expensive meal you can think of: wine and champagne and all the trimmings. You take care of the chef, the waiter, and keep the rest yourself."

"But you don't have to pay in advance," John protested.

"That's what you say," the man retorted. "But I am the kind of guy who today has it and tomorrow don't. And it may be that just when I can get the lady, I shouldn't have a buck. So I'm making sure."

A week went by, and he didn't show up. The second week he came in one afternoon and told John: "Tonight's the night. And don't forget the caviar. She is a Russian."

John continued the story: "That night he came with a luscious blonde, with lots of jewels. They got caviar and the best of everything: wine, champagne, cigars, cigarettes, everything. Then they get up and leave, and everybody bows to them, like he had an account with the hotel. All things paid, it comes to about sixty dollars, so I have forty dollars for myself. Not bad.

"A week later, the same fellow asks the doorman to call me out. He needed a shave, a haircut and a clean shirt, and looked as though he hadn't slept in a bed since I last saw him. 'Will you stake me to a dinner?' he asks. 'Sure. Come in. I still have some of your money.' 'Never mind that,' he says. 'I ain't fit to come in here. What I meant is stake me to dinner at the Automat.'

"I pulled out two five dollar bills and offered them to him. He took one and left. A month later, he came in spic and span, sat down, paid back the five dollars, and handed me another hundred dollar bill. 'I'll show up with her again some night. You did a fine job.' And he did show up with her again.

"After that, I never saw them again, That was twenty years ago. I still expect to see him come in needing a shave, a haircut, and a clean shirt, and ask me to stake him to a meal at the Automat. I'm sure he will, some day."

~

The late Frank Case rose from the bottom rung of the ladder to the topmost one in the hotel business. But his bellboys remained bellboys, elevator men stayed elevator men, and desk clerks remained desk clerks. Every job was practically a cul de sac. People who craved an opportunity to rise must have realized very quickly that hopes for advancement, if they existed at all, were very slim. Eventually, however, such men and women as preferred to stay put remained, and are still there: dishwashers, elevator operators, desk clerks, valets, headwaiters, and telephone operators. In the long run, they have all acquired satisfied miens which they present with an attitude of never having wanted anything better, or anything different.

This manner of running an organization, such as a hotel, worked profitably and satisfactorily, creating an air of stability and intimacy, and indirectly called forth the same degree of constancy in the clientele. The Algonquin is not only a hotel. It is a habit. There is no doubt that if faces had been continually changing at their posts, the Algonquin would never have acquired the atmosphere of home it now possesses.

In 1910, Nick Skundakis, a young Greek from the island of Crete, landed in New York and, since several of his compatriots were already working at the hotel, Nick was given a job. Nick wasn't twenty. He hadn't seen much of New York. A job was a job. The pay was satisfactory. He didn't know much English; probably no more than to understand at what floor to stop, but he stuck to his job as elevator man for six years, neat, smiling and willing. In the meantime, he married, and because another boy from Crete arrived who was willing to take his place, Nick was given the job as a room-service waiter: to carry up orders to the rooms: breakfast, cocktails in the afternoons, and such other services as people demanded.

Nick is still doing the same thing, after forty-two years. His hair, which was coal black, is silver white today, and America to him is represented by the twelve floors of the Algonquin, from the kitchen to the top, and the people of America are to Nick the people he sees at the hotel. "Americans," says Nick, "are good people; nice people. Generous people."

Nick has raised four children. Three sons participated in World War II "to defend this very nice, good country," and one of them was severely wounded. That, too, is part of Nick's world. "To fight for the America. His country. Yes sir. His country. I am American. My sons, Americans. Come war, my sons go to war. Sure. Good Americans all go to war. I am very proud. He got a medal and everything."

A whole world and two generations have passed him by. He can pronounce the most eminent names, and knows who was a writer of stories and who wrote plays. He has served the most famous actors and actresses; has seen them drunk and sober, happy and unhappy. Some of them have even borrowed money from him, and not all have paid him back. He knows each one's habits: how much cream in the tea, how much sugar in the coffee, how this one likes his eggs, that one his toast. He makes few mistakes, and believes himself on top of the world when an old client calls him by name and inquires how he feels: "The manager, he was angry with me sometime, long ago. He says everybody looks for Nick. Orders come from every room and people look for Nick, and Nick is nowhere. And what do you think happened?

"Mr. Fairbanks was alone in his room when I bring coffee, and he says, 'Sit down Nick, I want to talk to you.' And I say I got to go, and he says no, you stay, and he jumps out of bed and closes the door. 'You've got to listen.' What could I do? So I sit down and worry about orders and he talks and talks and talks, and I know nothing about what he talks, but he wants to talk and I say, 'Mr. Fairbanks, I've got to go. I've got orders. People waiting.' But he says no. He's got to talk. And I know nothing about what he says. He's got troubles. Big troubles. He's got to talk.

"Then he gives me ten dollars, and opens the door and says 'Thank you, Nick.' And I don't know why he says 'thank you' to me. When I come down, I catch hell. I explain. The manager asks what Mr. Fairbanks told me. I say 'I don't know what he told me. All I know is that he told me he is very sorry about something, but I don't know what.'

"Other people come and ask for breakfast: two eggs and coffee. I bring it up and go away. He rings again. He wants two more eggs and more coffee. And four times he rings the bell for more eggs and coffee. I ask who it is. They tell me he is a prizefighter: Firpo. Sometimes I come to a room and see man and wife, and one year later, the husband comes with another wife.

"I have seen everything," Nick says. "It is a big country with nice people. A very big country. This is a nice place to work. So many years. It's like yesterday."

"Didn't you ever want to do something else in the hotel?"

"Something else? What? I am room-service man. The best room-service man in the country.

"Man comes from Colorado and says to me: 'Are you Nick?' 'Yes,' I say, 'Sure.' And he says 'Mr. O'Brien he says to me, give regards to Nick. He is best room-service waiter.' Why another job? This is a good job; best job in the hotel. That's what I tell my boys. Get a job and stick to it. But you know, young people are so different. One day they want one thing, the next day they want something else. Too many new faces in the kitchen now. Five years, ten years, maybe they think they stay here too long and go look for another job."

There is Papa Mitchell, known to all the thousands who have passed through the lobby in the last thirty-eight years. Tall and stately, like a cross between a Southern senator and a minister, he has never missed a day in the thirty-eight years behind the desk. I remember him when his hair was black; it's iron-gray now. Affable, well-spoken, efficient, one would have thought when one first saw him at his desk that there was a man who would rise in the organization. But managers have come and gone, either because they failed or found better opportunities, and Mitchell is still there, and will probably still be there ten years from now, and as he has never had a thought of changing in the last thirty-eight years, he won't have one from now on.

"When I leave the Algonquin, it will be to retire to a farm. I couldn't work in another hotel. I'm married to the place. Mrs. Case used to tell me—she was a generous woman—'Mitchell, you are the Algonquin.' Where else would I have known such people as John Drew, De Wolf Hopper, Mencken, all the Barrymores, Eugene Walter, Ina Claire, Paul Armstrong, Teddy Roosevelt, Dr. Lyman Abbott, and so many others?"

And the stories he could tell, if he wanted or cared, of men risen from penury to affluence and down again. Actors who have become famous overnight: how one day they passed through the lobby unobserved and the next day saw people lined up from the elevator to the street to greet them. Playwrights, whose bills were piling up, and who by one stroke of fortune squared all the debts and laughingly told how fearful they were of passing Papa Mitchell's desk when the bills were unpaid.

Georges, the headwaiter, is no longer at the Algonquin. When he left, after thirty-five years, to better his condition, it seemed to many Algonquinites that nothing would ever be as it had been. His assistant, John, is now fulfilling the same functions, but nobody has ever really taken Georges's place. The headwaiters who followed him have only substituted for him. Though one had a feeling that Georges didn't have the best possible job or opportunity to which his education, upbringing, and manners entitled him, it was still good to see him. None of the steady guests at the Algonquin ever thought of Georges as a waiter, or a headwaiter, but more like a friend. Most of us go to see him in his new position.

John, born on the Dalmatian coast fifty years ago, and working at the Algonquin thirty years, has a wealth of stories about the famous and near famous. He tells how Mike Romanoff, Prince Romanoff to you, came in one day, ordered clams and roast beef, and after eating the clams, called John over, to tell him he had no money. John said, "Eat the roast beef, just the same." Six years later, having become affluent in Hollywood, he came to the Algonquin to pay his old bill.

John tells how a man said somebody had stolen his gold-handled umbrella, worth a hundred dollars, was compensated, and then somebody found the umbrella—worth two dollars.

"Did you tell him?"

"No. The customer is always right."

There is Miss Bush at the switchboard. She came to the Algonquin as a young girl, thirty-six years ago, on her first job, was stuck behind a switchboard, and has remained there ever since. She probably knows more about the Algonquin than even the owners ever knew, and knows as much about the management as anyone could. Many a night with Miss Bush on duty, some lonely writer or actor carries on a long conversation with her from his room, over the telephone, or comes down to talk to her. From this loneliest of professions, the writing of words, there suddenly arises a tremendous hunger for hearing oneself speak, and at such times, one looks for a sympathetic ear, and that Miss Bush has. How many plots of stories and plays has she not heard described? How many grievances has she listened to?

"She stole my best scene!"

"The manager took away my best lines."

"The director took the part away from me to give it to his girlfriend."

"It meant so much to me. I worked and worked and worked, and now it has all come to nothing."

"I told them, but nobody would believe me. All I needed was an opportunity, and I could show them: Look at Mary Martin. Nobody wanted her. She knocked at every door, and just because she put over one song, 'My Heart Belongs to Daddy,' look at her. That's what we girls need: an opportunity. Well, when I get mine, watch me climb! Thanks, Miss Bush. It was good to talk to you before going home to Kansas."

She has counted among her friends John Drew, who insisted her name was Rosy, Alice Brady, the Fairbankses, all the Barrymores, Irene Castle, Ruth Chatterton, Ina Claire, Marjorie Rambeau, Jeanne Eagels, Tallulah Bankhead, Gene Fowler, and van Loon. Mencken still comes down to her to have her fix his bow tie when he goes out to dinner. Edna Ferber never fails to have a chat with her. Dorothy Parker is an old friend. Miss Bush has a great collection of autographed books, and no Algonquinite playwright has ever missed giving her tickets for the first night of their play.

~

Any hotel that has functioned as long as the Algonquin has become a cosmos. There is not a room or suite that doesn't hold a multitude of interesting stories. What tragedies and comedies have been played out in them! The difference between most of the hotels and the Algonquin is that its cosmos held more individualities than individuals; that the tragedies, comedies, and joys were of a different nature; that the failure of a love story seemed more tragic than the failure of a love, and the failure of a play more tragic than a death in the family. The hotel has been a magnet that has attracted people who either have already distinguished themselves or are in the process of distinguishing themselves in their chosen professions, and thus they increase its magnetic power by magnetizing those who come in contact with it.

"It isn't true that artists are like other people. Artists are peculiar people. I know. I am an artist myself." Martin Kalaydjin, the valet of the Algonquin is an artist, a philosopher, and a psychologist. Born in Cesarea when it was Turkish Armenia, he came to the United States in 1922, and has been the valet of the hotel for the last ten years. He came here as an artist, a portrait painter, but after a few years of slow starvation, he apprenticed himself to a tailor.

"I could get a better job, earn more money in a bigger hotel. But in the winter, there are more mink coats in this small hotel than the biggest hotels. In the big hotel, maybe three thousand people come and go. You know nobody, they don't know you. Here I know the people and the people know me. In the big hotel, they call 'Valet!' I come. They give me clothes. When I bring them back they look at the bill, maybe tell me something I don't like, and say 'all right, valet.' Here they say 'Martin please,' and when I bring the clothes they say, 'How are you, Martin? Have a drink. How is your wife and child?' Maybe they tell me something about a story they're writing, or a play, or the part they are acting. Artists treat everybody like human beings: valet, waiters, everyone.

"Two actors, they live in the hotel for many years. Then they quarrel and don't speak for two years, but they send messages to each other by me. One day I say, 'Stop the foolishness,' and I say, 'Life is too short.'

They stop the foolishness, and both are now my best friends. They always give me tickets for first nights.

"Last year I go to Colorado for vacation, to paint a little. First person I meet is Mrs. Mary Chase, who wrote *Harvey*, and she tells me: 'Martin, come stay at my place; be my guest.' She introduces me to all her friends. I am an artist. She asks me what's up at the Algonquin, and I tell her. Same thing when I was in Hollywood. I meet Mr. Laughton on the street. He says 'Hello Martin. How are you?'

"All the people that come to the Algonquin, they know me, I know them. I go to the clothes closet and pick out myself what has to be pressed and bring it back when it is done. One actor has fifteen suits in the closet, but he wears only two, one brown and one blue. One day, the two suits are out to be cleaned and he sits in his room in his underwear and says he can't go out. I say, 'You've got thirteen more suits in the closet.' He says, 'Yes, but I don't like them. You can have them.'

"Artists are peculiar people, but nice humans in general, and generous and I like them because I am myself an artist. You know, you make a crease in an artist's sleeves and he's ready to shoot you, he gets so mad. But one minute later he is your best friend. When they come from Hollywood, they bring lots of clothes for me to clean. I am the first man they talk to when they come. 'Gee, it's good to be home and talk to you again. Have a drink. Sit down.'

"Marian Anderson, when she is away, she sends me all her gowns. Mr. Thurber, too, sends me bundles from Connecticut. 'Martin, take care,' they say.

"Somebody comes from far away, a friend of Mr. Sinclair Lewis, and he calls on me: 'Mr. Lewis, he says call Martin. He takes care of you. Speak to him when lonesome.' When Mr. Laughton comes back from Europe, he says, 'Sit down, Martin. I want to tell you something. I kissed the ground here when I came back.' And then he tells me all about Europe. He is a philosopher. He eats filet mignon three times a day, but he is a philosopher, and a little bit of a socialist . . . and a gourmet, first class. The waiter always tells the chef, 'This is for Mr. Laughton.' Mr. Ward Moorehouse, he too is a philosopher and a wonderful person. I take care of him, too.

"People say Mr. Case makes all the atmosphere of the Algonquin. I say no. I say everybody here makes the atmosphere. The elevator boys: Al Berthod, David Horty, and Tommy Rodriguez; the boys down in the scullery, in the kitchen, the waiters . . . everybody is the atmosphere, because everybody is interested in the people at the hotel. They all read papers. If a play, written by somebody they know, is a big success, everybody is happy and everybody goes to see it. If a play is a flop, everybody is unhappy, and when the playwright comes in, everybody ducks. Writers always give books autographed to me and others. When you had trouble last year with the trial and Mr. Chaplin, people you never saw, they all were interested, they all follow it. Atmosphere. What is it? Who makes it?

"I come from Cesarea. We have lots of honey there. You want to make a new beehive, you prepare conditions for the bees to come and you take a barrel, maybe put wax around it, and start. You make good conditions. Then the bees come. They make the hive. They make the honey. You only have to prepare for it. You don't make the honey. Mr. Case prepare conditions for artists to come to the hotel and like it: but he cannot do everything. Other people must help. Then the artists, like the bees, make the atmosphere, the honey, and the people in the kitchen, in the scullery and everybody else prepare conditions, like beehives. Some bees sting, like when you crease an actor's sleeve, or when he is accustomed to Boston scrod without paprika and the waiter brings scrod with paprika. But the same bee doesn't sting when you know what the bee wants. Take Peter Lorre. Nicest man. He talks nice and behaves nice, but when the clothes or the food not as he likes . . .

"I tell you, just plain people can be peculiar, too. One woman says, 'I give you a dollar if you give me button from Mr. Melvyn Douglas's coat.' Very peculiar. But I am an honest man. I give her a button from his coat and sew another button on. Another woman wants a necktie from another actor. I could give any necktie and say it's his, but I don't. I asked the actor for a necktie. I tell him what I want it for. One actor says give her any necktie and say it's from me. I say no. I'm no fetishist. This woman is. I give her necktie you wore or nothing. He laughs and gives me a tie. Men, too; they come from the South and the West and they want something that belongs to an actress maybe. Sometimes I can give, sometimes I say no. I will not take. I will not ask.

"This is a peculiar hotel, with peculiar people. And people like myself, in the kitchen, in the basement, become a little peculiar too, when they stay here long. When they go to other places to work, maybe to earn a little more money, they soon come back. They no longer can work other places where they don't know the people in the dining room and don't know most of the people in the rooms. People say the Algonquin is a home, not a hotel. But to make the place feel like a home, the people working in the hotel must feel it is a home for them, too. A job and a home."

And with this my story of the Algonquin is told.

Who's Who:
The Algonquin Guest List

Franklin P. Adams (1881–1960): American newspaper columnist, poet, and radio personality; his column, "The Conning Tower," launched careers and attracted such literary talent as Robert Benchley, Edna Ferber, John O'Hara, Dorothy Parker, and Edna St. Vincent Millay; a member of the Algonquin Round Table

Maude Adams (1872–1953): At one time America's most popular actress, best known for portraying Peter Pan on Broadway; a stage and lighting designer with three patents

George Ade (1866–1944): American writer, newspaper columnist, and playwright

Stella Adler (1901–1992): American actress in Yiddish theatre and on Broadway; a member of the famed Adler acting family, she became a highly influential acting teacher

Jack Alicoate (1918–1970): American editor and publisher of *Film Daily*, the industry's first daily newspaper

Marian Anderson (1897–1993): Celebrated American contralto, from opera to spirituals; involved in the civil rights movement, the first African-American to perform with the Metropolitan Opera

Sherwood Anderson (1876–1941): American novelist and short-story writer, including *Winesburg, Ohio* and best seller *Dark Laughter*

Joseph Anthony (1897–1991): American novelist, *The Gang* and *The Golden Village*

Michael Arlen (1895–1956): British essayist, short-story writer, novelist, playwright, and script writer

Tallulah Bankhead (1902–1968): American stage, screen, and radio actress playing nearly three hundred roles during her career; sometime guest at the Algonquin Round Table and resident of the hotel

Ethel Barrymore (1879–1959): Oscar-winning American stage, screen, and radio actress, part of the Barrymore family of actors

John Barrymore (1882–1942): American actor and member of the famed acting family, with acclaimed performances on stage, screen, and radio

Harold Bauer (1873–1951): American virtuoso violinist and pianist; debuted work by Brahms and Debussy, prolific recording artist; founder of the Beethoven Association

Rex Beach (1877–1949): American novelist and playwright, with multiple film adaptations of his work; Olympic water polo player

Menachem Begin (1913–1992): Israeli politician and founder of Likud who fought for Israel's independence as head of the Irgun; the sixth Prime Minister of Israel, Nobel Prize winner for peace treaty with Egypt in 1979

Robert Benchley (1889–1945): American newspaper columnist and humorist for the *New Yorker*; Oscar-winning (best short subject) humorist, film critic, actor, and director; one of the original members of the Algonquin Round Table

Richard Bennett (1870–1944): Prominent American stage and screen actor

Ben B. Bodne (1904–1992): Second owner of the Algonquin Hotel (1946–1987), maintaining its traditions and building on its success; previously a successful businessman in his native Charleston, South Carolina

Irene Bordoni (1885–1953): Popular Franco-American stage and screen actress and singer, most noted for premiering work by Cole Porter

Ernest Boyd (1887–1946): Irish-born essayist, biographer, and translator

Charles Brackett (1892–1962): American drama critic for the *New Yorker*, screenwriter and producer, collaborated with Billy Wilder on sixteen films, including *The Lost Weekend* and *Sunset Boulevard*

Heywood Broun Jr. (1888–1939): American journalist, columnist, editor for the *New York World*; active in political and labor issues; founded the Newspaper Guild; a member of the Algonquin Round Table

Ben Burman (1895–1984): American journalist and author, including his popular *Catfish Bend* series for both children and adults

Arthur Byron (1872–1943): American stage and film actor; founder and president of Actor's Equity Association

Louis Calhern (1895–1956): Academy Award–nominated American film and matinee idol stage actor

Benjamin Nathan Cardozo (1870–1938): American lawyer, jurist and Supreme Court justice, with a special interest in tort and contract law

Frank Case (1872–1946): American author and hotelier; moved from worker to manager then owner of the Algonquin Hotel (1902–1946), giving the hotel its name; catered to nearby journalists and theatrical talents, helping to establish the famed Round Table at the hotel

Vernon (1887–1918) and Irene Castle (1893–1969): Popular British-American husband-and-wife stage, vaudeville, and film dance team, popularized the foxtrot, ragtime, jazz, and African-American beats

Charlie Chaplin (1889–1977): Iconic English comic actor and filmmaker; the Tramp persona he created starred in such films as *The Gold Rush* and *Modern Times*; starred in *The Great Dictator*, for which author Konrad Bercovici sued and settled a plagiarism suit; cofounder United Artists

Ruth Chatterton (1882–1961): Oscar-nominated American stage, film, and television actress; best-selling novelist and transatlantic aviator

Ina Clair (1893–1985): American stage and film actress, appearing in multiple comedies on Broadway and alongside Greta Garbo in *Ninotchka*

Marc Connelly (1890–1980): Pulitzer Prize–winning American playwright, director, producer, and performer; a member of the Algonquin Round Table

John O'Hara Cosgrave (1866–1947): American author and editor, the *Wave* (San Francisco), *Collier's*, the *New York World*

Jane Cowl (1883–1950): American stage and film actress, playwright

Russell Crouse (1893–1966): American Pulitzer Prize–winning playwright, producer, and librettist for Broadway's Lindsay and Crouse

Bob Davis (1869–1942): American author, editor, globe-trotting columnist for the *Montreal Sun*, credited with discovering and encouraging such writers as O. Henry and Zane Grey

Vladimir de Pachmann (1848–1933): Russian-German concert pianist noted for playing Chopin and for his lively performance style

Melvyn Douglas (1901–1981): Academy, Tony, and Emmy Award–winning American film, theatre, and television actor; from suave leading man to his older character work, his notable films included *Ninotchka* with Greta Garbo and *Hud* with Paul Newman; active politically, married to Representative Helen Gahagan Douglas

Theodore Dreiser (1871–1945): Influential American novelist, poet, and journalist whose natural style and focus on poverty and ambition challenged acceptable morals of his day; notable novels, also made into films, include *An American Tragedy* and *Sister Carrie;* nominated for a Nobel Prize for Literature

John Drew (1853–1927): American stage actor and Broadway matinee idol, part of the Barrymore acting family

Jeanne Eagels (1890–1929): Academy Award–nominated American stage and film actress

Morris Ernst (1888–1976): Prominent American ACLU attorney, known for anti-censorship and pro-labor and civil liberties stance; defended *Ulysses* and Margaret Sanger

Douglas Fairbanks (1883–1939): American actor and Hollywood royalty, known for swashbuckling silent film roles; founding member of United Artists and the Motion Picture Academy; husband of actress Mary Pickford

Geraldine Farrar (1882–1967): American film actress and opera singer known for dramatic as well as vocal prowess, including first Metropolitan Opera performance of *Madame Butterfly*

William Faulkner (1897–1962): Celebrated Nobel, Pulitzer, National Book Award–winning American author of novels, short stories, and screenplays, often set in his native Mississippi

Edna Ferber (1885–1968): Pulitzer Prize–winning American novelist, short-story writer, and playwright, including *So Big*, *Showboat*, and *Giant*; a member of the Algonquin Round Table

Clyde Fitch (1865–1909): Popular American playwright of more than sixty plays, with major Broadway stars appearing in many of them

Henry James Forman (1879–1966): American author, book reviewer, editor of *Collier's* magazine

Gene Fowler (1890–1960): American journalist, best-selling author, and screenwriter

Greta Garbo (1905–1990): Academy Award–nominated Swedish-American film actress, a legend of classic Hollywood cinema for her performances in, among others, *Camille* and *Ninotchka*

Dr. Amadeo Gianini (1870–1949): Italo-American banker who founded the bank that became Bank of America

Margalo Gillmore (1887–1996): American stage, film, and television actress, creating roles on Broadway in plays by, among others, Eugene O'Neill and Clare Boothe Luce; from a noted acting family, including Frank Gillmore, founder of Actor's Equity; a member of the Algonquin Round Table

Montague Glass (1877–1934): British-American lawyer and writer noted for fictional duo Potash and Perlmutter, shedding a humorous light on the New York City garment center

Paulette Goddard (1910–1990): Academy Award–nominated American actress with a long and notable film career, including *Modern Times* and *The Great Dictator* with then-husband Charlie Chaplin

Leopold Godowsky (1870–1938): Lithuanian-American virtuoso pianist, composer, and teacher known for his two-century repertoire, innovative technique, and difficult transcriptions

Dr. Hyman Goldsmith (1907–1949): American nuclear physicist, one of many who advocated for more control of nuclear weapons

Clayton Hamilton (1881–1946): American drama critic, author, and university lecturer

Walter Hampden (1879–1955): American stage, film, and television actor, noted for his Cyrano and Shakespearian roles; president of the Players' Club

Elmer Harris (1878–1966): Prolific American playwright, screenwriter, and collaborator, most notably for *Johnny Belinda*

Ben Hecht (1894–1964): American novelist, journalist, playwright, director; successful, prolific Academy Award–winning screenwriter, including *Notorious, Wuthering Heights, The Front Page, His Girl Friday*, and *A Farewell to Arms*

Anna Held (1872–1918): Polish-French actress and singer; celebrated Broadway leading lady

Joe Hergesheimer (1880–1954): Popular and prolific American writer of short stories and novels, biographies, and history, many based in a wealthy, decadent milieu

Harry Hershfield (1895–1974): American cartoonist, columnist, and radio personality

Raymond Hitchcock (1865–1929): American silent film actor, Broadway stage actor, and producer

Samuel Hoffenstein (1890–1947): Russian-born American screenwriter, including *The Wizard of Oz* and *Phantom of the Opera*; poet and composer, collaborating with, among others, Cole Porter

Harry Houdini (born Erich Weisz, 1874–1926): Hungarian-American escape artist, magician and stunt performer, as well as a champion of debunking religious miracles

The Howard Brothers, Eugene (1883–1949) and Willie (1880–1965): Silesian-born Americans, among the earliest openly Jewish performers in vaudeville and Broadway musicals

Alice Hughes (1899–1977): American newspaper columnist and foreign correspondent on women's issues and fashion; hosted her own popular radio show

Fannie Hurst (1889–1968): Best-selling American novelist and short-story writer, one of the most widely read female authors of her time; supported and included current themes in her work, many of which became popular films

Elsie Janis (1889–1956): American stage and screen actor, singer, song-writer, and producer; one of the first American performers to entertain troops on foreign soil in World War I

Nunnally Johnson (1897–1977): Oscar-nominated American director, screenwriter, and/or producer of more than fifty notable films, including *The Man in the Gray Flannel Suit*, *Grapes of Wrath*, *The Three Faces of Eve*, and *The Dirty Dozen*; cofounder of International Pictures (1943)

Beatrice B. Kaufman (1885–1945): American writer and playwright; editor at Boni and Liveright of Hemingway, Steinbeck, and Faulkner; married to famed writer, director, and producer George S. Kaufman; a member of the Algonquin Round Table

George S. Kaufman (1889–1961): Every season from 1921 to 1958 had a Broadway show either written, directed, or produced by him, including Pulitzer Prize winners *Of Thee I Sing* and *You Can't Take It With You;* film adaptations include *Dinner at Eight, You Can't Take It With You;* a member of the Algonquin Round Table

Dr. Frank Kingdon (1884–1972): English-born journalist, activist, and educator, former minister and college president; chairman of a group that rescued thousands from the Holocaust

Sidney Kingsley (1906–1995): American Pulitzer Prize–winning playwright of *Men In White*, as well as multiple other plays and screenplays

Fiorella LaGuardia (1882–1947): Energetic, charismatic mayor of New York City and member of the House of Representatives; known for his friendship with and support for Franklin Delano Roosevelt and his New Deal reform principles

Hedy Lamarr (1914–2000): Austrian-American movie star in dozens of popular films; co-inventor of a torpedo radio guidance system utilized in World War II

Ring Lardner (1885–1933): American sports columnist, author, Broadway playwright, composer, and lyricist

Jesse Lasky (1880–1958): American film producer, including Hollywood's first feature film, *The Straw Man* and first Best Motion Picture–winner, *Wings;* founder of what would become Paramount Pictures; cofounder of the Academy of Recording Arts and Sciences

Charles Laughton (1899–1962): Academy Award–winning British actor of both modern and classic roles on Broadway and in Hollywood, including *Mutiny on the Bounty* and *The Hunchback of Notre Dame;* director, producer, and screenwriter

D. H. Lawrence (1885–1930): English writer known for such novels as *Lady Chatterley's Lover* and *Sons and Lovers,* plagued by controversy and censorship of his for-the-time sexually explicit work

Francis Lederer (1899–2000): Austro-Hungarian Empire-born American actor on Broadway, as well as in films alongside such stars as Ginger Rogers, John Barrymore, and Olivia de Havilland

Elmer Leterman (1887–1982): American insurance broker and author of best-selling books, including *The Sale Begins When the Customer Says No* and *The New Art of Selling*

Sinclair Lewis (1885–1951): Popular novelist and social critic, first American to win the Nobel Prize for Literature; critical of American capitalism and materialism, his best-known works include *Main Street, Babbitt, Dodsworth*, and *Elmer Gantry*

Kenneth Littauer (1894–1968): American journalist, war correspondent, and fiction editor at *Collier's*; literary agent of, among others, F. Scott Fitzgerald, Kurt Vonnegut, and James Salter; served in both world wars and was an early supporter of the Civil Air Patrol

Horace Liveright (1884–1933): American producer and publisher; cofounded Liveright and Boni and Liveright houses, and the Modern Library, publishing early work by such authors as Hemingway, Fitzgerald, Faulkner, Dreiser, Freud, Dorothy Parker, and Konrad Bercovici, as well as T. S. Elliot's *The Waste Land*

Otto "O. K." Liveright (1880–1944): American agent of, among others, Sherwood Anderson and Konrad Bercovici; brother of publisher Horace Liveright; active with the Provincetown Players as an actor, director, and playwright

Cissie Loftus (1893–1941): Scottish film and stage actress, singer, vaude-villian, and songwriter for various New York stage productions

Pauline Lord (1890–1950): American film and stage actress who created the lead role in Eugene O'Neill's *Anna Christie* on Broadway

Leonard Lyons (1906–1976): American nationally syndicated columnist of the "Lyon's Den" for the *New York Post*, covering performance, politics, and art, with a career total of 12,000 columns

Minnie Maddern (1865–1932): American actress and playwright who introduced Ibsen to the American public; a proponent of realism in acting, she took on the Theatrical Syndicate's control of plays and performers; also noted for her ASPCA animal rights work

Maurice Maeterlink (1862–1949): Nobel Prize–winning Belgian poet, essayist, and playwright, originally of the Symbolist movement; his theories of performance included working at one time with marionettes to express fate's control of man

Joseph Mankiewicz (1909–1993): Academy Award–winning American director, screenwriter, and producer of dozens of major studio films, including *A Letter to Three Wives, All About Eve, Cleopatra, Guys and Dolls, Suddenly Last Summer*, and *No Way Out*, which introduced actor Sidney Poitier

Richard Mansfield (1857–1907): English actor and theatrical manager and producer, celebrated for performances of Shakespeare on Broadway, Gilbert and Sullivan with the D'Oyly Carte, and *Dr. Jekyll and Mr. Hyde* in London and New York

Queen Marie of Romania (1875–1938): Born into the British royal family, the last Queen of Romania as wife of King Ferdinand I; successful proponent of a Greater Romania, doubling her kingdom in size at the Paris Peace Conference; subject of many scandals in her personal life; author and, briefly, *New York World* columnist

H. L. Mencken (1880–1956): American journalist, essayist, and satirist of his day's cultural and social scene; known as "the sage of Baltimore," he was eminently quotable and had a deep circle of literary friends; his numerous books include studies of government, language, and Nietzsche, whom he greatly admired

Edna St. Vincent Millay (1892–1950): Pulitzer Prize–winning American poet, author, and playwright; helped establish The Cherry Lane Theatre in Greenwich Village; used her poetry to explore women's issues, as well as to champion the war effort in World War II

Marilyn Miller (1898–1936): Popular American Broadway actress, singer, and dancer, a former Ziegfeld girl, her rags-to-riches characters appeared with, among others, Will Rogers, W. C. Fields, and Eddie Cantor; her brief film career included costarring with Fred Astaire

Ward Morehouse (1895–1966): American playwright, screenwriter, columnist, and critic, known for lively celebrity interviews, notably twenty-five years of his "Broadway After Dark Column" for the *New York Sun*

Mae Murray (1885–1965): American actress, producer, and screenwriter, a former Ziegfeld girl who became a major star on Broadway, as well as in film, opposite the likes of Valentino and John Gilbert

George Jean Nathan (1882–1958): American drama critic and editor, worked closely with H. L. Mencken as cofounders of influential literary magazines the *American Spectator* and the *American Mercury*; had a long relationship with actress Lillian Gish

Robert Nathan (1894–1985): American poet and author of novels *The Bishop's Wife*, *Portrait of Jennie*, and *One More Spring*, all turned into highly successful films, as well as writing screenplays for such films as *The Clock*; his cousins included poet Emma Lazarus and Supreme Court Justice Benjamin Cardozo

Alla Nazimova (1879–1945): Russian-American actress, screenwriter, and producer, a major star on Broadway in Ibsen, Turgenev, and Chekhov; under her own Nazimova Productions, she directed and starred in films she produced, as well as designing lighting and costumes

Dudley Nichols (1895–1960): American director and Academy Award–winning screenwriter; a founder of the Screenwriters Guild, he wrote or cowrote scripts for such classic films as *Bringing Up Baby, Stagecoach, For Whom the Bell Tolls*, and *The Bells of St. Mary's*

Louis Nizer (1902–1994): American lawyer, best-selling author, and artist, representing many celebrities and high-profile cases, including Johnny Carson, Mae West, Salvador Dali, and Konrad Bercovici's successful plagiarism suit against Charlie Chaplin for *The Great Dictator;* source for Broadway's *A Case of Libel*

Frank Norris (1870–1902): American journalist and author, his work often focused on corporate corruption, while also displaying some of his own racism and anti-Semitism; adaptations for stage and screenplays include films starring Valentino and directed by D. W. Griffith and Erich von Stroheim

Edward O'Brien (1890–1941): American editor, poet, and anthologist of acclaimed *Best American Short Stories* annual series, including multiple multi-starred stories by Konrad Bercovici; O'Brien also authored books about poetry, as well as the defining *Son of the Morning: Portrait of Nietzsche*

Paul O'Dwyer (1907–1998): Irish-born influential American politician, serving as president of the New York City Council; opposed library censorship, supported freedom of speech, labor unions, and civil rights issues

Eugene O'Neill (1888–1953): Nobel, Pulitzer, and Tony Award–winning American playwright celebrated for his realism in such works as *Long Day's Journey Into Night, Emperor Jones, Desire Under the Elms*, and *The Iceman Cometh*; associated through his early sea plays with the Provincetown Players; a sometime resident and neighbor of Konrad Bercovici in Ridgefield, Connecticut

Ignacy Paderewski (1860–1941): World-renowned Polish virtuoso pianist and composer; a vocal advocate for Polish independence, he eventually became Poland's prime minister and a signer of the Versailles Peace Treaty ending World War I; his philanthropy included public monuments and setting up benefits for musicians

Dorothy Parker (1893–1967): Popular American humorist, poet, critic, and Academy Award–nominated co-screenwriter of the original *A Star Is Born*, known for her sharp, highly quotable comments; founding member of the Algonquin Round Table

Anna Pavlova (1881–1931): Russian prima ballerina, the first to tour the world with her own company, including a groundbreaking inclusion of ethnic dances in her otherwise classic, romantic-style repertoire

Jack Pickford (1893–1933): Canadian-American actor, director, and producer who appeared in more than 130 films, often as the all-American boy next door; brother of silent-film star Mary Pickford

Luigi Pirandello (1867–1936): Italian novelist, short-story writer, and Nobel Prize–winning playwright, whose plays were also adapted for film by such directors as Vittorio de Sica; originally a vocal Italian nationalist, he eventually questioned Fascism under Mussolini

Martin Quigley (1890–1964): American publisher and editor, acquired and merged various trade papers to form *Motion Picture Daily;* coauthored the Motion Picture Production Code aka the Hays Code reflecting his own conservative Catholic beliefs

Marjorie Rambeau (1889–1970): Academy Award–nominated American film and Broadway stage actress

Burton Rascoe (1892–1957): American author, magazine and newspaper publisher, editor, and literary critic; his popular *New York Tribune* syndicated column appeared in four hundred newspapers

Elmer Rice (1892–1967): Pulitzer Prize–winning American playwright who broke from stage conventions with *Street Scene* and *The Adding Machine*, with some successful adaptations for film; actively supported the ACLU and P.E.N.; served as president of the Dramatists Guild

John Rogge (1903–1981): American attorney who investigated graft, fraud, and Nazi issues for the U.S. government; his support for free speech and liberal causes, questioning of HUAC and Justice Department cover-ups, ended up putting him at odds with Washington

Elliott Roosevelt (1910–1990): American writer, aviation official, and brigadier general during World War II, flying reconnaissance missions and identifying potential base sites, utilizing new night aerial photography; accompanied his father, FDR, on various diplomatic meetings

Eleanor Roosevelt (1884–1962): The longest-serving First Lady, redefining the role as an activist for civil, women's, and youth rights; a diplomat and our first delegate to the UN; admired for her public service and followed by millions in popular columns and radio shows; arranged Marian Anderson's famed performance at the Lincoln Memorial

Elmer Roper (1900–1971): American pioneer in market research and public polling, cofounding one of the first market research companies based on scientific sampling utilized by, among others, FDR; syndicated radio and newspaper columnist

Harold Ross (1892–1951): American journalist, cofounder and editor-in-chief of the *New Yorker*; an original member of the Algonquin Round Table, attracting such talent as Alexander Woollcott, James Thurber, E. B. White, Dorothy Parker, Robert Benchley, Vladimir Nabokov, John O'Hara, and J. D. Salinger

Lillian Russell (1860–1922): Foremost American actress and singer of her day in vaudeville, operettas, and musicals on Broadway and in England; known for her charisma and style, notably the first voice carried over long-distance telephone lines

William Saroyan (1908–1981): Pulitzer Prize– and Academy Award–winning Armenian-American novelist, playwright, and short-story writer known for his depiction of immigrant life in California, including *The Time of Your Life*, *My Heart's in the Highlands*, and *My Name Is Aram*, as well as several memoirs and many essays

Clare Sheridan (1879–1970): English writer and sculptress, with such famous sitters as Lenin and Trotsky; European correspondent for the *New York World*; a cousin of Winston Churchill

Robert Sherwood (1896–1955): Pulitzer Prize– and Academy Award–winning American playwright and screenwriter of, among others, *The Bishop's Wife*, *The Best Years of Our Lives*, and *Rebecca*; one of the original members of the Algonquin Round Table, formed with fellow *Vanity Fair* staff members Dorothy Parker and Robert Benchley

Alexander Smallens (1889–1972): Russian-American conductor and musical director of several major cities' orchestras and organizations, as well as on Broadway, notably for the premiere and various tours and revivals of Gershwin's *Porgy and Bess*

Bernard Sobel (1887–1964): American playwright, drama critic for the *New York Daily Mirror* and author of books on the theatre; as a publicist, his clients included Florenz Ziegfeld and theatre owners and producers Lee, Sam, and Jacob Shubert

E. H. Sothern (1859–1933): American actor from an acting family, known for his romantic leading roles; he was also considered one of the finest Shakespearean actors of his day both on Broadway and on extensive tours

Laurence Stallings (1894–1968): American author, playwright, screenwriter, and book reviewer at the *New York World*, introduced to the Round Table by fellow staff members Deems Taylor and Heywood Broun; a wounded veteran in World War I, his experiences inspired Broadway hit *What Price Glory?* and his Pulitzer Prize–nominated novel *Plumes*

Vilhjalmur Stefansson (1879–1962): Canadian Arctic explorer, who organized major expeditions and published archaeological and anthropological studies on them; an Explorers Club member, he was also associated with experimental dietary issues, including an all-meat diet

Gertrude Stein (1874–1946): American novelist, poet, and playwright whose Paris salon helped launch Matisse, Picasso, and Cezanne, among others, and attracted such writers as Hemingway, Fitzgerald, James Joyce, and Konrad Bercovici; her *The Autobiography of Alice B. Toklas* was a bestseller

Rabindranath Tagore (1861–1941): Nobel Prize–winning Bengali poet, internationally acclaimed in all literary genres, including novels, plays, and short stories; composer, songwriter, and painter; influential social reformer and educator

Deems Taylor (1885–1966): American music critic for the *New York World*, popular composer; a classical music proponent and broadcast commentator, his extensive work for Disney's classic film *Fantasia* included choosing pieces and speaking on the soundtrack itself; a member of the Algonquin Round Table

Laurette Taylor (1883–1946): American silent film and stage actress known for her more natural, spontaneous acting style in such major Broadway productions as Tennessee Williams's *The Glass Menagerie*; also starred in popular film versions of several stage plays

Dorothy Thompson (1883–1961): Influential American journalist and syndicated columnist, one of the few women radio broadcasters of her time; the first journalist to be thrown out of Nazi Germany, her commentary on Europe and the start of World War II are noted for their historical significance

John Toohey (1879–1946): American journalist, playwright, and publicist; as a member of the Algonquin Round Table, cited as having provided the name for the *New Yorker* when the new magazine was being brainstormed there over lunch

Arthur Tracy (1899–1997): Internationally acclaimed American singer and actor, known for his romantic style on stage, radio, and in film, performing alongside, among others, Bing Crosby and Kate Smith; a popular recording artist, his version of *Pennies From Heaven* was used in the 1981 film of that name

Jim Tully (1886–1947): American prize fighter and journalist, initially known for his critiques of Hollywood celebrities; his rough-and-tumble life and bold style led to critically acclaimed and commercially successful novels, plays, and autobiographies

Lenore Ulric (1892–1970): American actress, starring on Broadway and in silent and early sound films; managed and directed by famed producer David Belasco for most of her stage career, she specialized in critically acclaimed femme fatale roles

Rudolph Valentino (1895–1926): Italian actor and dancer whose silent Hollywood films made him an iconic sex symbol; followed everywhere by the press and female fans, his films such as *The Sheik* and *Four Horsemen of the Apocalypse* helped change the look of male leads; his early death at age thirty-two heightened his legendary status

Hendrik Willem van Loon (1882–1944): Dutch-American journalist, author, and illustrator of his own work; a popular historian, he was best known for his *Story of the World*, intended for children, as well as numerous other books focusing on historical events and the arts

Bayard Veiller (1869–1943): American playwright, screenwriter, producer, and film director whose Broadway hits included *The 13th Chair* as well as *Within the Law*, with multiple adaptations of his work for film

Jimmy Walker (1881–1946): American politician known for his flamboyant presence as New York State senator, state assemblyman, and mayor of New York City (1926–1932); his championing of social issues and condemnation of the Ku Klux Klan led to working-class support; his corrupt Tammany Hall association led to his resignation

Edgar Wallace (1875–1932): Highly prolific British author of hundreds of stories, screenplays, and crime thrillers, with more than 50 million copies sold of his work, more than 160 films made from it, including *King Kong* and *On the Spot*, credited with launching Charles Laughton's career

Lew Wallace (1827–1905): American author of *Ben Hur*, the influential, best-selling novel of the nineteenth century and source for the film of the same name; his many other books, mainly historical adventures, were often based on his experiences as a Civil War general, politician, and diplomat

Eugene Walter (1874–1941): American playwright of numerous works, including *Paid in Full* and *The Easiest Way*, many of which were turned into films; screenwriter for various additional studio films in Hollywood

H. G. Wells (1866–1946): British author, best known for his science fiction and utopian works, including *The Time Machine* and *War of the Worlds*; highly prolific historian and guest columnist for the *New York World*

Rebecca West (1892–1983): Widely read British author and journalist for, among others, *The [London] Times*, the *New Yorker* and the *New Republic*, receiving a CBE and a DBE from England for her contributions to the arts; noted for her war coverage and as a spokeswoman for feminist and social causes; a member of the Algonquin Round Table

Earl Wilson (1907–1987): American syndicated columnist and author, known for his inside info on celebrities and Broadway during the theatre's so-called golden years

Peggy Wood (1892–1978): Popular American stage, film, and television actress; Emmy-nominated for hit TV series *Mama;* Academy-Award nominated and Golden-Globe winner for *The Sound of Music;* author, playwright, and president of ANTA; a member of the Algonquin Round Table

Alexander Woollcott (1887–1943): Author, playwright, and drama critic for the *New York Times,* the *New Yorker,* and the *New York World;* first prominent columnist to become a radio storyteller and commentator with his "Town Crier" show; a member of the Algonquin Round Table

Elinor Wylie (1885–1928): American poet and novelist, critically praised for her polished yet emotional style; poetry editor at *Vanity Fair* and the *New Republic;* her short eight-year career produced four novels, four volumes of poetry, and a significant number of magazine articles

Index

Thurber, James, 150
Toklas, Alice, 24
Tolstoy, Leo, 11
  "amateur" productions of, 19
Tone, Franchot, 83
Toscanini, Arturo, 44
Touhey, John, 3
Tournament of Champions, the,
  54–55, 134
Tracy, Arthur, 54
Tridon, Andre, 93–95
Trotsky, Leon, 94
Truman, Harry S., 6
Tully, Jim, 83–85
Twain, Mark, 102
21 (NYC club), 118
Two Blind Mice, 115

Ulrich, Lenore, 17
Undercover (Bercovici), xvi
Updike, John, xv

Valentino, Rudolph, 100, 119–24, 129
van Loon, Hendrik Willem, 28, 31,
  83, 148
  at Algonquin, 28–29, 33, 35–36,
    44, 60
  attraction to Algonquin, 19
  Case on, 27
  death of, 142
  egotism of, 80
  many talents of, 29
  as quipster, 3
van Noppen, Leonard Charles, 92
Veiller, Bayard, 78
Verlaine, Paul-Marie, xvi, 61
Versailles conference, 85
Victor Hugo (restaurant), 102
"Vieux Colombier Theatre," 11
Virginia Glasses, the, 118

Vogue, 26

Walker, Jimmy, 70
Wallace, Edgar, 18–19
Wallace, Lew, 15
Wallack's, 15
Walter, Eugene, 75–77, 147
War Department, the, 29, 138
Wave, The, 13
Wells, H. G., 66, 83
West, Rebecca, 122
Whitman, Walt, 93
Widor, Charles Maria, xii, 74
Wilson, Earl, 70–71
Wilson, Woodrow, 85
Winslow, Thamster, 31
Woman's Home Companion, xiv
Wood, Peggy, 16, 111
Woollcott, Alexander, 11
  as actor, 4
  "atmosphere" around, 111
  and Broun, 70
  and Case, 24
  as critic, 3, 14, 66, 69, 130
  fearlessness of, 3
  laughter of, 53
  Panaite on, 130
  as Round Table regular, 18, 65, 69,
    106
World, The, xiii
World War I, 16, 30, 85, 98–99,
  122–23
World War II, xi, xvi, 4, 78, 145
Wylie, Elinor, 126–27

Young, Loretta, 118

Zale, Tony, 55
Zamacois, Eduardo, 139
Ziegfeld Jr., Florenz, 139